FAMILY FOOTY QUIZ BOOK!

FROM THE MAKERS OF THE UK'S BIGGEST-SELLING FOOTBALL MAGAZINE

D1322515

NO CHEATING!

BBC Books, an imprint of Ebury Publishing 20 Vauxhall Bridge Road
London SW1V 2SA

BBC Books is part of the Penguin Random House group of companies
whose addresses can be found at global.penguinrandomhouse.com

Penguin
Random House
UK

First published by BBC Books in 2020

www.penguin.co.uk

A CIP catalogue record for this book is available from the British Library

ISBN 9781785946349

Commissioning editor: Albert DePetrillo
Project editor: Daniel Sorensen
Production: Phil Spencer
Printed and bound in Great Britain by Clays Ltd, Elcograf S.p.A

Penguin Random House is committed to a sustainable future for our
business, our readers and our planet. This book is made from
Forest Stewardship Council® certied paper

Match of the Day Magazine is published by Immediate Media Company
London Limited under licence from BBC Studios

PAZ! KETCH!

WELCOME!

You hold in your hands Match of the Day magazine's
Family Footy Quiz Book – the ultimate test of football knowledge, with
1,000 questions for you to tackle. By the end of it you will know, once and
for all, who your family's No.1 footy expert really is. Good luck, quizzers!

IT'S ALMOST TIME FOR KICK-OFF!

HOW TO PLAY!

- You need two players – one under-16 and one adult. Or you could
  form two teams – but it needs to be under-16s versus adults!
- You all need a pen or pencil and you need a brain bursting with footy knowledge!
- There are 16 rounds of questions and 500 points each up for grabs.
  At the end of each quiz, add up how many correct answers you get!
- The winner – the player who scores the most points – can then officially
  claim to be the king or queen of footy knowledge in your house!

MY FACT FILE!

My name: _____ My age: _____

My home town: _____

My favourite team: _____

My favourite player: _____

MATCH of the DAY magazine

FAMILY FOOTY QUIZ BOOK!

CONTENTS

PREMIER LEAGUE

A WHOLE NEW

PART ONE

The Prem is in a league of its own – with some of the biggest clubs, most iconic players and most magical moments in football history. Who knows more about the world's greatest league? Let battle commence, quizzers!

LEAGUE OF NATIONS!

Q Which international teams do these Premier League stars and heroes play for?

1 SADIO MANE

SENEGAL	✓
NIGERIA	
IVORY COAST	

2 RICHARLISON

BRAZIL	✓
PARAGUAY	
COLOMBIA	

3 PHILIP BILLING

CZECH REPUBLIC	
DENMARK	✓
AUSTRALIA	

4 YOURI TIELEMANS

BELGIUM	✓
FRANCE	
HOLLAND	

5 YERRY MINA

ITALY	
COLOMBIA	
CHILE	✓

6 FABIAN SCHAR

AUSTRIA	
GERMANY	
SWITZERLAND	✓

7 JOSH KING

SCOTLAND	
NORWAY	✓
AUSTRALIA	

8 LUKA MILIVOJEVIC

SERBIA	✓
CROATIA	
SLOVENIA	

9 JAN BEDNAREK

POLAND	
RUSSIA	
CZECH REPUBLIC	✓

ANSWERS ON P153 **MY SCORE** /9

LEAGUE OF NATIONS!

Q Which international teams did these Premier League legends and cult heroes play for?

1 JUAN SEBASTIAN VERON

- CHILE
- ARGENTINA ✓
- MEXICO

2 ALEXANDER HLEB

- BELARUS
- BULGARIA ✓
- GEORGIA

3 GEREMI

- BRAZIL
- CAMEROON ✓
- SOUTH AFRICA

4 JUAN PABLO ANGEL

- MEXICO
- COLOMBIA
- PARAGUAY ✓

5 DAVOR SUKER

- CROATIA ✓
- SERBIA
- TURKEY

6 SAMI HYYPIA
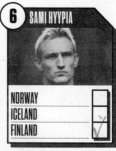
- NORWAY
- ICELAND
- FINLAND ✓

7 PAULO WANCHOPE

- PERU
- ECUADOR ✓
- COSTA RICA

8 LUCAS RADEBE

- MALI
- ZIMBABWE ✓
- SOUTH AFRICA

9 MARIANS PAHARS

- UKRAINE
- LATVIA ✓
- CZECH REPUBLIC

GOAL KINGS CROSSWORD!

Q Use the clues to fill in the crossword – the theme is Prem goalscorers!

ACROSS

2 Richarlison's Prem club before he moved to Everton (7)
5 The other English club Mohamed Salah has played for (7)
7 Liverpool and Senegal hotshot, _____ Mane (5)
9 The home stadium of England superstar Marcus Rashford (3,8)
10 Country of Arsenal striker Pierre-Emerick Aubameyang (5)

DOWN

1 The winner of the Premier League Golden Boot in 2016 and 2017 (5,4)
3 The Football League club Jamie Vardy left to join Leicester (9)
4 Home country of Wolves' star striker Raul Jimenez (6)
6 Sergio Aguero's first European club, _____ Madrid (8)
8 Chelsea striker Kevin Oghenetega Tamaraebi Bakumo-_____ (7)

ANSWERS ON P153   **MY SCORE** [ ] /10

GOAL KINGS CROSSWORD!

Q Use the clues to fill in the crossword – the theme is Prem goalscorers!

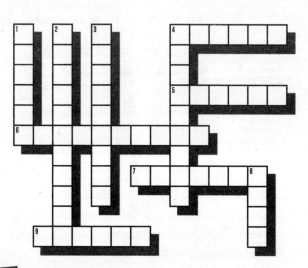

ACROSS

4 First club of Arsenal legend Thierry Henry (6)
5 Joint 1997-98 Golden Boot winner, Chris _____ (6)
6 Club that signed Ruud van Nistelrooy from Man. United (4,6)
7 Prem Golden Boot winner Robin van Persie played for this country (7)
9 Surname of French striker who bagged for six prem clubs, Nicolas _____ (6)

DOWN

1 PFA Young Player of the Year in 1995 and 1996, Robbie _____ (6)
2 Alan Shearer began his career at this club (11)
3 Joined Liverpool in 1995 for an English record fee of £8.5m, Stan _____ (9)
4 Didier Drogba joined Chelsea from this European club (9)
8 First name of another joint 1997-98 Golden Boot winner _____ Dublin (4)

PFA

TEAM OF THE YEAR TEASERS

Q Here are the last four Prem Teams of the Year – name the missing players!

1 2018-19

EDERSON
MAN. CITY

TRENT ALEXANDER-ARNOLD
LIVERPOOL

VIRGIL VAN DIJK
LIVERPOOL

A A.L.
MAN. CITY

ANDREW ROBERTSON
LIVERPOOL

B B.S.
MAN. CITY

FERNANDINHO
MAN. CITY

C P.P.
MAN. UNITED

D R.S.
MAN. CITY

SERGIO AGUERO
MAN. CITY

SADIO MANE
LIVERPOOL

A

B

C

D

2 2017-18

DAVID DE GEA
MAN. UNITED

A K.W.
MAN. CITY

B N.O.
MAN. CITY

JAN VERTONGHEN
TOTTENHAM

C M.A.
CHELSEA

DAVID SILVA
MAN. CITY

D C.E.
TOTTENHAM

KEVIN DE BRUYNE
MAN. CITY

MOHAMED SALAH
LIVERPOOL

HARRY KANE
TOTTENHAM

SERGIO AGUERO
MAN. CITY

A

B

C

D

3 2016-17

DAVID DE GEA
MAN. UNITED

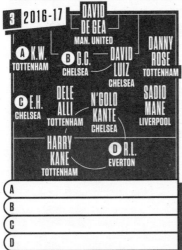

A K.W.
TOTTENHAM

B G.G.
CHELSEA

DAVID LUIZ
CHELSEA

DANNY ROSE
TOTTENHAM

C E.H.
CHELSEA

DELE ALLI
TOTTENHAM

N'GOLO KANTE
CHELSEA

SADIO MANE
LIVERPOOL

HARRY KANE
TOTTENHAM

D R.L.
EVERTON

A

B

C

D

4 2015-16

DAVID DE GEA
MAN. UNITED

A H.B.
ARSENAL

B T.A.
TOTTENHAM

WES MORGAN
LEICESTER

DANNY ROSE
TOTTENHAM

C R.M.
LEICESTER

DELE ALLI
TOTTENHAM

N'GOLO KANTE
LEICESTER

D D.P.
WEST HAM

HARRY KANE
TOTTENHAM

JAMIE VARDY
LEICESTER

A

B

C

D

ANSWERS ON P153 **MY SCORE** /16

PFA
TEAM OF THE YEAR TEASERS

Q Here are four classic Prem Teams of the Year – name the missing players!

1 1994-95

- **A** T.F. — BLACKBURN
- **B** R.J. — LIVERPOOL
- **C** G.P. — MAN. UNITED
- COLIN HENDRY — BLACKBURN
- GRAEME LE SAUX — BLACKBURN
- MATT LE TISSIER — SOUTHAMPTON
- PAUL INCE — MAN. UNITED
- TIM SHERWOOD — BLACKBURN
- **D** J.K. — TOTTENHAM
- ALAN SHEARER — BLACKBURN
- CHRIS SUTTON — BLACKBURN

A _____
B _____
C _____
D _____

2 1998-99

- **A** N.M. — LEEDS
- GARY NEVILLE — MAN. UNITED
- **B** S.C. — TOTTENHAM
- JAAP STAM — MAN. UNITED
- DENIS IRWIN — MAN. UNITED
- DAVID BECKHAM — MAN. UNITED
- **C** E.P. — ARSENAL
- PATRICK VIEIRA — ARSENAL
- **D** D.G. — TOTTENHAM
- DWIGHT YORKE — MAN. UNITED
- NICOLAS ANELKA — ARSENAL

A _____
B _____
C _____
D _____

3 2001-02

- **A** S.G. — NEWCASTLE
- STEVE FINNAN — FULHAM
- RIO FERDINAND — LEEDS
- **B** S.H. — LIVERPOOL
- **C** W.B. — SOUTHAMPTON
- **D** R.P. — ARSENAL
- ROY KEANE — MAN. UNITED
- PATRICK VIEIRA — ARSENAL
- RYAN GIGGS — MAN. UNITED
- RUUD VAN NISTELROOY — MAN. UNITED
- THIERRY HENRY — ARSENAL

A _____
B _____
C _____
D _____

4 2008-09

- EDWIN VAN DER SAR — MAN. UNITED
- **A** G.J. — PORTSMOUTH
- RIO FERDINAND — MAN. UNITED
- **B** N.V. — MAN. UNITED
- PATRICE EVRA — MAN. UNITED
- CRISTIANO RONALDO — MAN. UNITED
- STEVEN GERRARD — LIVERPOOL
- RYAN GIGGS — MAN. UNITED
- **C** A.Y. — ASTON VILLA
- **D** N.A. — CHELSEA
- FERNANDO TORRES — LIVERPOOL

A _____
B _____
C _____
D _____

BEAT THE CLOCK! START•STOP 01:00 MIN SEC

Q You've got 60 seconds to answer as many questions about the Prem as you can!

1 Which club did Jurgen Klopp manage before he took charge at Liverpool?

2 Which ledge striker is the top scorer in Premier League history?

3 Which country does Everton forward Bernard play for?

4 Sheffield United paid £20m to sign which striker in August 2019?

5 Which Premier League club plays its home games at St Mary's Stadium?

6 Which Prem club was Juan Mata signed to between 2011-14?

7 If The Eagles were playing against The Seagulls, what would the match be?

8 Which club has won the Premier League the most times?

9 Thierry Henry is the record Premier League goalscorer for which club?

10 Tottenham star Dele Alli began his career with which Football League club?

ANSWERS ON P153 **MY SCORE** ☐ /10

BEAT THE CLOCK

START•STOP

01:00

MIN | SEC

Q You've got 60 seconds to answer as many questions about the Prem as you can!

1 Which player scored the first goal in Premier League history back in 1992?

....

2 Which Premier League club did Italian striker Fabrizio Ravanelli play for from 1996-97?

....

3 Which Prem club went unbeaten for the whole of the 2003-04 season?

....

4 Who was manager of Blackburn when they won the Premier League in 1994-95?

....

5 Michael Owen left Liverpool to sign for which club in 2004?

....

6 Which country did Prem Golden Boot winner Jimmy Floyd Hasselbaink play for?

....

7 Which Premier League club used to play its home games at Maine Road?

....

8 Which club did Tony Yeboah play for in the Premier League from 1995-97?

....

9 Which Prem club's shirt was sponsored by O2 from 2002 to 2006?

....

10 Christian Gross managed which Premier League club between 1997 and 1998?

....

ANSWERS ON P153 **MY SCORE** /10

GOLDEN BOYS!

Q Here are the Golden Boot winners from the last ten years of the Premier League – all you need to do is fill in the blanks!

SEASON	TOP SCORER	CLUB	GOALS
2009-10	DIDIER DROGBA	_chelsea_	29
2010-11	CARLOS TEVEZ DIMITAR BERBATOV	MAN. CITY _weckham_	20
2011-12	ROBIN VAN PERSIE	_DTD_	30
2012-13	_____	MAN. UNITED	26
2013-14	_____	LIVERPOOL	31
2014-15	_____	MAN. CITY	26
2015-16	_____	TOTTENHAM	25
2016-17	_____	TOTTENHAM	29
2017-18	_____	LIVERPOOL	32
2018-19	P. AUBAMEYANG _Mane_ MOHAMED SALAH	ARSENAL LIVERPOOL LIVERPOOL	22

ANSWERS ON P153   **MY SCORE** [ ] **/10**

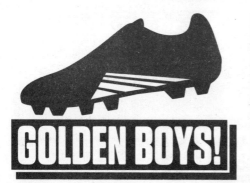

GOLDEN BOYS!

SEASON	TOP SCORER	CLUB	GOALS
1992-93	TEDDY SHERINGHAM	NOTT'M FOREST & _____	22
1993-94	ANDY COLE	_____	24
1994-95	_____	BLACKBURN	34
1995-96	ALAN SHEARER	_____	31
1996-97	_____	NEWCASTLE	25
1997-98	CHRIS SUTTON DION DUBLIN _____	BLACKBURN COVENTRY LIVERPOOL	18
1998-99	MICHAEL OWEN DWIGHT YORKE JIMMY FLOYD HASSELBAINK	LIVERPOOL MAN. UNITED _____	18
1999-2000	KEVIN PHILLIPS	_____	30
2000-01	_____	CHELSEA	23
2001-02	_____	ARSENAL	24

ANSWERS ON P153 **MY SCORE** ___ /10

PREMIER LEAGUE
PERFORMERS!

Q 15 of these clubs have played in the Premier League since it was launched back in 1992 – but do you know which ones?

ANSWERS ON P153   **MY SCORE**   /15

PREMIER LEAGUE
F O U N D E R S !

Q 15 of these clubs were in the Premier League for its first-ever season way back in 1992-93 – but do you know which ones?

1

2

3

4

5

6

7

8

9

10

11

12

13

14

15

16

17

18

19

20

WORLD CUP

It's the greatest show on earth. An epic month-long festival of football. A time for heroes, drama and unforgettable lifelong memories. But how much do you know about the FIFA World Cup? Let's find out, quizzers!

RUSSIA PUZZLER!

Q These talented footballers all appeared at the 2018 World Cup in Russia – but do you remember which country they played for?

1 ALAN DZAGOEV

SERBIA
UKRAINE
RUSSIA

2 DIEGO GODIN

URUGUAY
PARAGUAY
COLOMBIA

3 RAPHAEL GUERREIRO

MEXICO
PANAMA
PORTUGAL

4 THOMAS DELANEY

AUSTRALIA
USA
DENMARK

5 JUAN CUADRADO

ITALY
COLOMBIA
CHILE

6 CORENTIN TOLISSO

AUSTRIA
ITALY
FRANCE

7 HIRVING LOZANO

PERU
SWEDEN
MEXICO

8 RICARDO RODRIGUEZ

SERBIA
SWITZERLAND
SPAIN

9 ADNAN JANUZAJ

POLAND
BELGIUM
CROATIA

ANSWERS ON P153 **MY SCORE** /9

USA '94 FLASHBACK!

Q These retro footballers played at the 1994 World Cup in the USA – but do you remember which country they played for?

1 EMIL KOSTADINOV

BULGARIA ☐
USA ☐
RUSSIA ☐

2 TONI POLSTER

NORWAY ☐
DENMARK ☐
AUSTRIA ☐

3 FREDDY RINCON

MEXICO ☐
COLOMBIA ☐
SOUTH AFRICA ☐

4 GHEORGHE POPESCU

RUSSIA ☐
BULGARIA ☐
ROMANIA ☐

5 VALERI KARPIN

BULGARIA ☐
ROMANIA ☐
RUSSIA ☐

6 DANIEL AMOKACHI
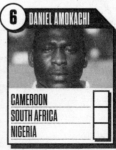
CAMEROON ☐
SOUTH AFRICA ☐
NIGERIA ☐

7 ARIEL ORTEGA

MEXICO ☐
ARGENTINA ☐
URUGUAY ☐

8 ALAIN SUTTER

SWITZERLAND ☐
FRANCE ☐
AUSTRIA ☐

9 JONAS THERN

NORWAY ☐
SWEDEN ☐
DENMARK ☐

WORLD CUP WINNERS!

Q Can you name the World Cup winner, Golden Boot winner and hosts of these five tournaments?

YEAR	WINNER	HOST NATION
2018		RUSSIA
2014	GERMANY	
2010		SOUTH AFRICA
2006	ITALY	
2002	BRAZIL	& SOUTH KOREA

YEAR	GOLDEN BOOT WINNER	COUNTRY
2018		ENGLAND
2014	JAMES RODRIGUEZ	
2010	THOMAS MULLER	
2006	MIROSLAV KLOSE	
2002	RONALDO	

ANSWERS ON P153   **MY SCORE** ☐ /10

WORLD CUP WINNERS!

Q Can you name the World Cup winner, Golden Boot winner and hosts of these five tournaments?

YEAR	WINNER	HOST NATION
1998		FRANCE
1994	BRAZIL	
1990	WEST GERMANY	
1986		MEXICO
1982		SPAIN

YEAR	GOLDEN BOOT WINNER	COUNTRY
1998		CROATIA
1994	OLEG SALENKO / HRISTO STOICHKOV	RUSSIA
1990		ITALY
1986		ENGLAND
1982		ITALY

ANSWERS ON P153   **MY SCORE** ☐ /10

WORLD CUP
FINAL LOSERS!

Q Can you fill in the name of the losing countries in these four World Cup finals?

1 — 2014 WORLD CUP FINAL

DATE: **13 JULY 2014**
VENUE: **MARACANA STADIUM, RIO**
ATTENDANCE: **74,738**
REFEREE: **NICOLA RIZZOLI** (ITALY)

ROMERO
ZABALETA — DEMECHELIS — GARAY — ROJO
PEREZ — MASCHERANO — BIGLIA — LAVEZZI
MESSI
HIGUAIN

GERMANY 1-0

2 — 2010 WORLD CUP FINAL

DATE: **11 JULY 2010**
VENUE: **SOCCER CITY, JOHANNESBURG**
ATTENDANCE: **84,490**
REFEREE: **HOWARD WEBB** (ENGLAND)

STEKELENBURG
VAN DER WEIL — HEITINGA — MATHIJSEN — VAN BRONCKHORST
VAN BOMMEL — DE JONG
ROBBEN — SNEIJDER — KUYT
VAN PERSIE

0-1 **SPAIN**

3 — 2006 WORLD CUP FINAL

DATE: **9 JULY 2006**
VENUE: **OLYMPIC STADIUM, BERLIN**
ATTENDANCE: **69,000**
REFEREE: **HORACIO ELIZONDO** (ARGENTINA)

BARTHEZ
SAGNOL — THURAM — GALLAS — ABIDAL
VIEIRA — MAKELELE
RIBERY — ZIDANE — MALOUDA
HENRY

ITALY 1-1

ITALY WIN 5-3 ON PENALTIES

4 — 2002 WORLD CUP FINAL

DATE: **30 JUNE 2002**
VENUE: **INTERNATIONAL STADIUM, YOKOHAMA** ATTENDANCE: **69,029,**
REFEREE: **PIERLUIGI COLLINA** (ITALY)

KAHN
LINKE — RAMELOW — METZELDER
FRINGS — HAMANN — JEREMIES — BODE
SCHNEIDER
NEUVILLE — KLOSE

0-2 **BRAZIL**

ANSWERS ON P153 **MY SCORE** /4

WORLD CUP
FINAL LOSERS!

Q Can you fill in the name of the losing countries in these four World Cup finals?

1 1998 WORLD CUP FINAL

DATE: **12 JULY 1998**
VENUE: **STADE DE FRANCE, PARIS**
ATTENDANCE: **80,000**
REFEREE: **SAID BELQOLA** (MOROCCO)

TAFFAREL
CAFU — ALDAIR — JUNIOR BAIANO — R. CARLOS
CESAR SAMPAIO — DUNGA
RIVALDO — LEONARDO
BEBETO — RONALDO

0-3 — **FRANCE**

2 1994 WORLD CUP FINAL

DATE: **17 JULY 1994**
VENUE: **ROSE BOWL, PASADENA, USA**
ATTENDANCE: **94,194**
REFEREE: **SANDOR PUHL** (HUNGARY)

PAGLIUCA
MUSSI — BARESI — MALDINI — BENARRIVO
D. BAGGIO — ALBERTINI
BERTI — DONADONI
R. BAGGIO — MASSARO

BRAZIL — **0-0**

BRAZIL WIN 3-2 ON PENALTIES

3 1978 WORLD CUP FINAL

DATE: **25 JUNE 1978**
VENUE: **ESTADIO MONUMENTAL, BUENOS AIRES** ATTENDANCE: **71,483**
REFEREE: **SERGIO GONELLA** (ITALY)

JONGBLOED
KROL
JANSEN — BRANDTS — POORTVLIET
NEESKENS — HAAN — W. VAN DE KERKHOF
R. VAN DE KERKHOF — RENSENBRINK
REP

ARGENTINA — **3-1**

4 1962 WORLD CUP FINAL

DATE: **17 JUNE 1962**
VENUE: **ESTADIO NACIONAL, SANTIAGO**
ATTENDANCE: **68,679**
REFEREE: **NIKOLAY LATYSHEV** (SOVIET UNION)

SCHROJF
TICHY — POPLUHAR — PLUSKAL — NOVAK
KVASNAK
POSPICHAL — MASOPUST
JELINEK — KADRABA
SCHERER

BRAZIL — **3-1**

ANSWERS ON P153 — **MY SCORE** — **/4** — motdmag.com **29**

BEAT THE CLOCK

START•STOP
01:00
MIN SEC

Q You've got 60 seconds to answer as many World Cup questions as you possibly can!

1 Which country has lifted the World Cup the most times?

....

2 Which European country knocked England out of the 2018 World Cup?

....

3 What nationality is all-time World Cup top scorer Miroslav Klose?

....

4 England famously won the World Cup in which year – 1958, 1966 or 1974?

....

5 Which Germany baller scored the winning goal in the 2014 World Cup final?

....

6 Who is the only player to win the World Cup three times?

....

7 Which MOTD ledge scored a hat-trick against Poland at the 1986 World Cup?

....

8 Which Italy defender was headbutted by Zinedine Zidane in the 2006 final?

....

9 In which year did Lionel Messi make his World Cup finals debut – 2002, 2006 or 2010?

....

10 Who was named player of the tournament at the 2018 World Cup in Russia?

....

ANSWERS ON P153   **MY SCORE** [ ] /10

BEAT THE CLOCK → START•STOP 01:00 MIN SEC

Q You've got 60 seconds to answer as many World Cup questions as you possibly can!

1 Which country won the first World Cup tournament back in 1930?

2 When was the last time a non-European country lifted the World Cup trophy?

3 Geoff Hurst scored three in England's 4-2 World Cup final win – who scored the other?

4 Who scored the winner from the penalty spot in the 1990 World Cup final in Italy?

5 Which player scored a record 13 goals at a single World Cup in 1958?

6 Which Argentina striker was the top scorer at the 1978 World Cup?

7 Which two European countries have won the World Cup four times?

8 Which singer missed a penalty in the opening ceremony of the 1994 World Cup?

9 Who was the manager of the Republic Of Ireland at the 1994 World Cup in the USA?

10 Who scored an extra-time winning goal in the 2010 World Cup final in South Africa?

ANSWERS ON P153 **MY SCORE** ☐ **/10**

WORLD CUP KEEPERS!

Q These giant figures have all played in goal at a World Cup tournament – but which country did they play for?

1 IGOR AKINFEEV

UKRAINE
POLAND
RUSSIA

2 CLAUDIO BRAVO

COLOMBIA
COSTA RICA
CHILE

3 DANIJEL SUBASIC

CROATIA
SERBIA
BOSNIA

4 YANN SOMMER

AUSTRIA
SWITZERLAND
GERMANY

5 JIM LEIGHTON

ENGLAND
SCOTLAND
REPUBLIC OF IRELAND

6 BODO ILLGNER

DENMARK
HOLLAND
GERMANY

7 CLAUDIO TAFFAREL

ITALY
BRAZIL
SWEDEN

8 ROBIN OLSEN

SWEDEN
DENMARK
NORWAY

9 FERNANDO MUSLERA

URUGUAY
TURKEY
ITALY

ANSWERS ON P153   **MY SCORE** [ ] /9

HAT-TRICK HEROES!

Q These superstar strikers all scored memorable hat-tricks at a World Cup – but which country were they playing for?

1 GONZALO HIGUAIN

FRANCE
ARGENTINA
ITALY

2 PAULETA

BRAZIL
PORTUGAL
ANGOLA

3 OLEG SALENKO

BULGARIA
ROMANIA
RUSSIA

4 TOMAS SKUHRAVY

CZECHOSLOVAKIA
ROMANIA
POLAND

5 PREBEN ELKJAER

SWEDEN
DENMARK
NORWAY

6 JUST FONTAINE

FRANCE
BELGIUM
ITALY

7 SANDOR KOCSIS

BULGARIA
HOLLAND
HUNGARY

8 ZBIGNIEW BONIEK

RUSSIA
POLAND
CZECH REPUBLIC

9 TEOFILO CUBILLAS

PERU
CHILE
SPAIN

ANSWERS ON P153 **MY SCORE** /9

CHAMPIONS LEAGUE

The Champions League is the most prestigious football competition in the world, throwing together the titans of European football. Since its launch in 1992, we've been wowed by insane matches, incredible goals and iconic displays – how much do you know about it, quizzers?

CHAMPIONS MAP!

Q Can you find the 12 Champions League-winning clubs on the map below?

1	AC & INTER MILAN		5	BORUSSIA DORTMUND		9	LIVERPOOL	
2	AJAX		6	CHELSEA		10	MAN. UNITED	
3	BARCELONA		7	REAL MADRID		11	MARSEILLE	
4	BAYERN MUNICH		8	JUVENTUS		12	PORTO	

ANSWERS ON P153 **MY SCORE** /12

CHAMPIONS MAP!

Q Can you find the 12 stadiums that have hosted a final of the Champions League?

1	MILLENNIUM STADIUM		5	STADIO OLIMPICO		9	NOU CAMP	
2	ESTADIO DA LUZ		6	ALLIANZ ARENA		10	STADE DE FRANCE	
3	SAN SIRO		7	LUZHNIKI STADIUM		11	ATATURK OLYMPIC	
4	WANDA METROPOLITANO		8	HAMPDEN PARK		12	NSC OLIMPIYSKIY	

LEGENDARY
LINE-UPS!

Q Which Champions League-winning teams are laid out in these team formations below?

1 2006-07 UCL FINAL

DATE: **23 MAY 2007**
VENUE: **OLYMPIC STADIUM, ATHENS**
ATTENDANCE: **63,000**
REFEREE: **HERBERT FANDEL** (GERMANY)

2-1 LIVERPOOL

2 2005-06 UCL FINAL

DATE: **17 MAY 2006**
VENUE: **STADE DE FRANCE, PARIS**
ATTENDANCE: **79,610**
REFEREE: **TERJE HAUGE** (NORWAY)

2-1 ARSENAL

3 2009-10 UCL FINAL

DATE: **22 MAY 2010**
VENUE: **SANTIAGO BERNABEU, MADRID**
ATTENDANCE: **73,490**
REFEREE: **HOWARD WEBB** (ENGLAND)

BAYERN MUNICH **0-2**

4 2011-12 UCL FINAL

DATE: **19 MAY 2012**
VENUE: **ALLIANZ ARENA, MUNICH**
ATTENDANCE: **62,500**
REFEREE: **PEDRO PROENCA** (PORTUGAL)

BAYERN MUNICH **1-1** WIN 4-3 ON PENALTIES

ANSWERS ON P153   **MY SCORE** ☐ /4

LEGENDARY
LINE-UPS!

Q Which Champions League-winning teams are laid out in these team formations below?

1 1994-95 UCL FINAL

DATE: **24 MAY 1995**
VENUE: **ERNST HAPPEL STADIUM, VIENNA**
ATTENDANCE: **49,730**
REFEREE: **ION CRACIUNESCU** (ROMANIA)

VAN DER SAR
REIZIGER | BLIND | RIJKAARD | F. DE BOER
SEEDORF | DAVIDS
LITMANEN
FINIDI | OVERMARS
R. DE BOER

1-0 AC MILAN

2 1997-98 UCL FINAL

DATE: **20 MAY 1998**
VENUE: **AMSTERDAM ARENA, AMSTERDAM**
ATTENDANCE: **48,500**
REFEREE: **HELLMUT KRUG** (GERMANY)

ILLGNER
PANUCCI | SANCHIS | HIERRO | CARLOS
REDONDO
KAREMBEU | SEEDORF
RAUL
MORIENTES | MIJATOVIC

JUVENTUS **0-1**

3 2003-04 UCL FINAL

DATE: **26 MAY 2004**
VENUE: **VELTINS ARENA, GELSENKIRCHEN**
ATTENDANCE: **53,053**
REFEREE: **KIM MILTON NEILSEN** (DENMARK)

BAIA
FERREIRA | COSTA | CARVALHO | VALENTE
COSTINHA
MENDES | MANICHE
DECO
CARLOS ALBERTO | DERLEI

MONACO **0-3**

4 1992-93 UCL FINAL

DATE: **26 MAY 1993**
VENUE: **OLYMPIC STADIUM, MUNICH**
ATTENDANCE: **64,400**
REFEREE: **KURT ROTHLISBERGER** (SWITZERLAND)

BARTHEZ
ANGLOMA | BOLI | DESAILLY
EYDELIE | SAUZEE | DI MECO
DESCHAMPS
PELE | VOLLER
BOKSIC

AC MILAN **0-1**

CAREER PATH

Q Can you name the Champions League superstars from their epic career history?

PLAYER 1
- 2006-08 ZNICZ PRUSZKOW
- 2008-10 LECH POZNAN
- 2010-14 BORUSSIA DORTMUND
- 2014-PRESENT BAYERN MUNICH

PLAYER 2
- 2005-06 NACIONAL
- 2006-07 GRONINGEN
- 2007-11 AJAX
- 2011-14 LIVERPOOL
- 2014-PRESENT BARCELONA

PLAYER 3
- 1995-2001 PARMA
- 2001-18 JUVENTUS
- 2018-19 PSG
- 2019-PRESENT JUVENTUS

PLAYER 4
- 2005-07 ROSARIO CENTRAL
- 2007-10 BENFICA
- 2010-14 REAL MADRID
- 2014-15 MAN. UNITED
- 2015-PRESENT PSG

ANSWERS ON P153 **MY SCORE** /4

CAREER PATH

Q Can you name the Champions League legends from their epic career history?

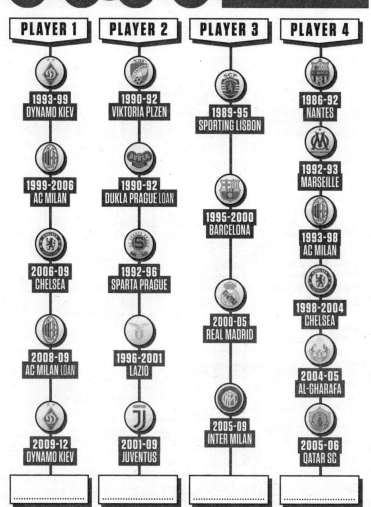

PLAYER 1

1993-99
DYNAMO KIEV

1999-2006
AC MILAN

2006-09
CHELSEA

2008-09
AC MILAN LOAN

2009-12
DYNAMO KIEV

PLAYER 2

1990-92
VIKTORIA PLZEN

1990-92
DUKLA PRAGUE LOAN

1992-96
SPARTA PRAGUE

1996-2001
LAZIO

2001-09
JUVENTUS

PLAYER 3

1989-95
SPORTING LISBON

1995-2000
BARCELONA

2000-05
REAL MADRID

2005-09
INTER MILAN

PLAYER 4

1986-92
NANTES

1992-93
MARSEILLE

1993-98
AC MILAN

1998-2004
CHELSEA

2004-05
AL-GHARAFA

2005-06
QATAR SC

FINAL FANTASY!

Q These megastar ballers have hit the net in the biggest game of them all – a Champions League final! But for which team did they score?

1 PEDRO

REAL MADRID ☐
BARCELONA ☐
CHELSEA ☐

2 ALVARO MORATA

ATLETICO MADRID ☐
CHELSEA ☐
JUVENTUS ☐

3 LUIS SUAREZ

BARCELONA ☐
AJAX ☐
LIVERPOOL ☐

4 ARJEN ROBBEN

BAYERN MUNICH ☐
REAL MADRID ☐
CHELSEA ☐

5 DIEGO MILITO

INTER MILAN ☐
ATLETICO MADRID ☐
AC MILAN ☐

6 DIDIER DROGBA

MARSEILLE ☐
CHELSEA ☐
BAYERN MUNICH ☐

7 DIEGO GODIN
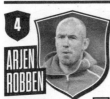

ATLETICO MADRID ☐
INTER MILAN ☐
VALENCIA ☐

8 MARIO MANDZUKIC

JUVENTUS ☐
BAYERN MUNICH ☐
INTER MILAN ☐

9 ILKAY GUNDOGAN
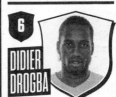

BORUSSIA DORTMUND ☐
MAN. CITY ☐
BAYER LEVERKUSEN ☐

ANSWERS ON P153 **MY SCORE** ☐ /9

FINAL FANTASY!

Q These megastar ballers have hit the net in the biggest game of them all – a Champions League final! But for which team did they score?

1
BASILE BOLI

MARSEILLE ☐
AC MILAN ☐
MONACO ☐

2
DANIELE MASSARO

JUVENTUS ☐
AC MILAN ☐
PARMA ☐

3
JARI LITMANEN

BARCELONA ☐
AJAX ☐
LIVERPOOL ☐

4
LARS RICKEN

AJAX ☐
BORUSSIA DORTMUND ☐
BAYER LEVERKUSEN ☐

5
PREDRAG MIJATOVIC

BAYERN MUNICH ☐
REAL MADRID ☐
AC MILAN ☐

6
STEVE McMANAMAN

LIVERPOOL ☐
MAN. UNITED ☐
REAL MADRID ☐

7
ZINEDINE ZIDANE

JUVENTUS ☐
REAL MADRID ☐
BORDEAUX ☐

8
XABI ALONSO

LIVERPOOL ☐
REAL MADRID ☐
BAYERN MUNICH ☐

9
DMITRI ALENICHEV

BAYER LEVERKUSEN ☐
PORTO ☐
INTER MILAN ☐

ANSWERS ON P153 **MY SCORE** ☐ /9

BEAT THE CLOCK

START•STOP `01:00` MIN SEC

Q You've got 60 seconds to answer as many UCL questions as you possibly can!

1 Which European club has won the Champions League the most times?

....

2 Which footy megastar is the top scorer in Champions League history?

....

3 Which country does electric Bayern Munich forward Serge Gnabry play for?

....

4 Who was manager of Man. United the last time they won the Champions League?

....

5 Which English stadium hosted the Champions League final in 2011 and 2013?

....

6 Who scored Liverpool's second goal in the 2019 UCL final against Tottenham?

....

7 Jose Mourinho has won the UCL twice – with Porto in 2004 and which club in 2010?

....

8 Which British club has won the Champions League the most times?

....

9 Which Wales baller scored in both the 2014 and 2018 Champions League finals?

....

10 Which was the last French club to reach the final of the Champions League?

....

ANSWERS ON P153 **MY SCORE** ☐ **/10**

BEAT THE CLOCK

START•STOP

01:00

MIN SEC

Q You've got 60 seconds to answer as many UCL questions as you possibly can!

1 Which club was the winner of the first Champions League in 1993?

....

2 Which stadium hosted the 1999 final between Man. United and Bayern Munich?

....

3 Which Scottish midfielder won the Champions League with Borussia Dortmund in 1997?

....

4 Who was manager of Leeds when they reached the UCL semi-finals in 2001?

....

5 Which English ref took charge of the 2016 UCL final between Real and Atletico Madrid?

....

6 Who was manager of Chelsea when they won the competition back in 2012?

....

7 Which was the last Italian club to win the Champions League?

....

8 Patrick Kluivert scored the winner in the 1995 UCL final for which club?

....

9 Which Arsenal keeper was sent off in the 2006 UCL final against Barcelona?

....

10 Who was the last Englishman to score in a Champions League final?

....

ANSWERS ON P153   **MY SCORE** [   ] **/10**

2019-20
L I N E - U P S !

Q Which Champions League clubs lined up with these players during the 2019-20 season?

1

LOPES

DENAYER   MARCELO   MARCAL

DUBOIS   TOUSART   GUIMARAES   CORNET

EKAMBI   DEMBELE   AOUAR

....

2

ONANA

MAZRAOUI   VELTMAN   BLIND   TAGLIAFICO

MARTINEZ   VAN DE BEEK

NERES   ZIYECH   PROMES

TADIC

....

3

OBLAK

TRIPPIER   SAVIC   FELIPE   LODI

KOKE   PARTEY   NIGUEZ   LEMAR

MORATA   CORREA

....

4

OSPINA

DI LORENZO   MANOLAS   MAKSIMOVIC   RUI

ALLAN

CALLEJON — FABIAN — ZIELINSKI — INSIGNE

MERTENS

....

ANSWERS ON P153   **MY SCORE**   /4

LEGENDARY
LINE-UPS!

Q Which Champions League clubs lined up with these players during the competition's history?

1

KAHN

SAGNOL KUFFOUR KOVAC LIZARAZU

HARGREAVES JEREMIES

EFFENBERG

SANTA CRUZ ELBER SERGIO

....

2

BUFFON

THURAM TUDOR MONTERO BIRINDELLI

ZAMBROTTA TACCHINARDI DAVIDS NEDVED

DEL PIERO TREZEGUET

....

3

BARTHEZ

MARTIN CHRISTANVAL DIAWARA LEONARD

DJETOU COLLINS

BERNABIA

IKPEBA TREZEGUET HENRY

....

4

MARCHEGIANI

NEGRO MIHAJLOVIC NESTA PANCARO

SENSINI VERON

CONCECIAO SALAS NEDVED

INZAGHI

....

TRANSFERS

Ever since Willie Groves made a record-breaking £100 move from West Brom to Aston Villa in 1893, football fans around the world have been obsessed with superstar signings and big-money moves. This round will test your transfer knowledge to the max, quizzers!

TRANSFER RECORD PUZZLER!

Q Here are the ten biggest transfers in football history – can you name the players?

PLAYER	FROM	TO	YEAR	FEE
1_____	BARCELONA	PSG	2017	£198m
2_____	MONACO	PSG	2018	£165m
3_____	CHELSEA	REAL MADRID	2019	£150m
4_____	LIVERPOOL	BARCELONA	2018	£142m
5_____	B. DORTMUND	BARCELONA	2017	£135m
6_____	BENFICA	ATLETICO MADRID	2019	£114m
7_____	ATLETICO MADRID	BARCELONA	2019	£107m
8_____	JUVENTUS	MAN. UNITED	2016	£89m
9_____	REAL MADRID	JUVENTUS	2018	£88m
10_____	TOTTENHAM	REAL MADRID	2013	£86m

ANSWERS ON P153 **MY SCORE** ☐ /10

TRANSFER RECORD PUZZLER!

Q Here are the ten biggest transfers of the 1990s and 2000s – can you name the players?

PLAYER	FROM	TO	YEAR	FEE
1_____	MAN. UNITED	REAL MADRID	2009	£80m
2_____	INTER MILAN	BARCELONA	2009	£56m
3_____	AC MILAN	REAL MADRID	2009	£56m
4_____	JUVENTUS	REAL MADRID	2001	£46.6m
5_____	BARCELONA	REAL MADRID	2000	£37m
6_____	PARMA	LAZIO	2000	£35m
7_____	PARMA	JUVENTUS	2001	£32.6m
8_____	VALENCIA	LAZIO	2001	£29m
9_____	LAZIO	MAN. UNITED	2001	£28.1m
10_____	LAZIO	INTER MILAN	1999	£28m

ANSWERS ON P153 **MY SCORE** ☐ /10

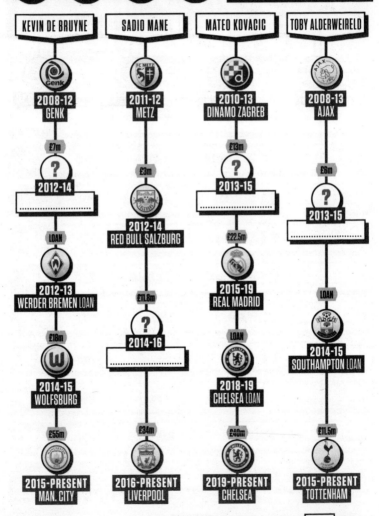

CAREER PATH

Q Can you fill in the missing clubs from the big-money moves of these stars?

KEVIN DE BRUYNE

2008-12 GENK

£7m
? 2012-14
....

LOAN
2012-13 WERDER BREMEN LOAN

£18m
2014-15 WOLFSBURG

£55m
2015-PRESENT MAN. CITY

SADIO MANE

2011-12 METZ

£3m
2012-14 RED BULL SALZBURG

£11.8m
? 2014-16
....

£34m
2016-PRESENT LIVERPOOL

MATEO KOVACIC

2010-13 DINAMO ZAGREB

£13m
? 2013-15
....

£22.5m
2015-19 REAL MADRID

LOAN
2018-19 CHELSEA LOAN

£40m
2019-PRESENT CHELSEA

TOBY ALDERWEIRELD

2008-13 AJAX

£6m
? 2013-15
....

LOAN
2014-15 SOUTHAMPTON LOAN

£11.5m
2015-PRESENT TOTTENHAM

ANSWERS ON P153 **MY SCORE** ☐ /4

CAREER PATH

Q Can you fill in the missing clubs from these old-school Premier League moves?

EMMANUEL PETIT

1988-97
MONACO

£2.5m

1997-2000
ARSENAL

£7m

?
2000-01
....

£7.5m

2001-04
CHELSEA

NICKY BUTT

1992-2004
MAN. UNITED

£2.5m

?
2004-10
....

LOAN

2005-06
BIRMINGHAM LOAN

FREE

2010-11
SOUTH CHINA

JAMIE REDKNAPP

1990-91
BOURNEMOUTH

£350k

1991-2002
LIVERPOOL

FREE

?
2002-05
....

FREE

2005
SOUTHAMPTON

WIM JONK

1986-1988
VOLENDAM

UNKNOWN

1988-1993
AJAX

UNKNOWN

1993-1995
INTER MILAN

UNKNOWN

1995-1998
PSV

£2.5m

?
1998-2000
....

FOOTBALL LEAGUE

Away from the bright lights and celebrity ballers of the Prem is the world of wonder we call the Football League. From sleeping giants in the Championship to the plucky little scrappers of League Two, the second, third and fourth tiers of English football provide drama, excitement and passion. But are you an expert? Let's find out, quizzers!

BADGE
BAMBOOZLER!

1

HUDDERSFIELD
WIGAN
PRESTON

2

STOKE
SUNDERLAND
SWINDON

3

CARDIFF
DERBY
LUTON

4

CHARLTON
BRISTOL CITY
READING

5

SUNDERLAND
STOKE
LINCOLN

6

PORTSMOUTH
BIRMINGHAM
SHEFFIELD WEDNESDAY

7

BRISTOL CITY
MIDDLESBROUGH
BARNSLEY

8

GRIMSBY
PLYMOUTH
CARDIFF

9

SHEFFIELD WEDNESDAY
IPSWICH
COVENTRY

ANSWERS ON P153   **MY SCORE** /9

BADGE BAMBOOZLER!

Q Which Football League clubs do these badges belong to?

1

SALFORD
MILLWALL
WALSALL

2

DERBY
OXFORD
BURTON

3

LUTON
BARNSLEY
ROCHDALE

4

SOUTHEND
GILLINGHAM
TRANMERE

5

MIDDLESBROUGH
LEYTON ORIENT
CREWE

6

COLCHESTER
MILLWALL
SHREWSBURY

7

GRIMSBY
SOUTHEND
MORECAMBE

8

COVENTRY
OLDHAM
BRADFORD

9

AFC WIMBLEDON
ACCRINGTON STANLEY
HULL

ANSWERS ON P153   **MY SCORE** /9

LOCATION, LOCATION, LOCATION!

Q Can you locate all six Football League clubs on the map below?

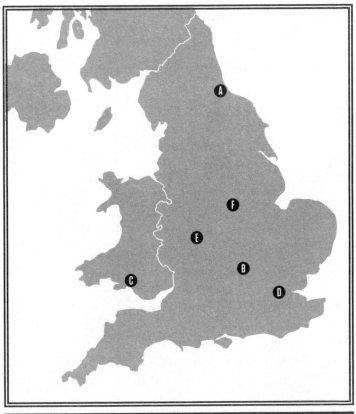

1	SWANSEA		3	BIRMINGHAM		5	NOTTINGHAM FOREST	
2	MIDDLESBROUGH		4	CHARLTON		6	LUTON	

ANSWERS ON P153   **MY SCORE** ☐ /6

LOCATION, LOCATION,
LOCATION!

Q Can you locate all six Football League clubs on the map below?

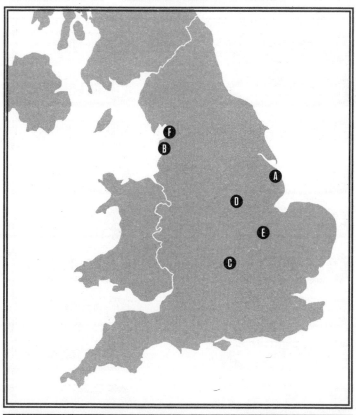

1	MANSFIELD		3	PETERBOROUGH		5	BLACKPOOL
2	MK DONS		4	MORECAMBE		6	GRIMSBY

THE NICKNAME GAME!

Q Can you match each of these Football League teams to their club nickname?

1 PORTSMOUTH		**A** THE TIGERS
2 SUNDERLAND		**B** THE MILLERS
3 ROTHERHAM		**C** THE TROTTERS
4 HULL		**D** THE POTTERS
5 DERBY		**E** THE BLACK CATS
6 FULHAM		**F** THE ROYALS
7 STOKE		**G** POMPEY
8 SWANSEA		**H** THE SWANS
9 READING		**I** THE RAMS
10 BOLTON		**J** THE COTTAGERS

ANSWERS ON P153 **MY SCORE** ☐ /10

THE NICKNAME GAME!

Q Can you match each of these Football League teams to their club nickname?

1. SWINDON
2. BRADFORD
3. EXETER
4. MANSFIELD
5. MORECAMBE
6. SOUTHEND
7. PLYMOUTH
8. NORTHAMPTON
9. WALSALL
10. LINCOLN

A. THE PILGRIMS
B. THE IMPS
C. THE SADDLERS
D. THE SHRIMPERS
E. THE SHRIMPS
F. THE ROBINS
G. THE STAGS
H. THE GRECIANS
I. THE COBBLERS
J. THE BANTAMS

ANSWERS ON P153 **MY SCORE** /10

FOOTBALL LEAGUE SUPERSTARS!

Q These ballers have all been named in a PFA Football League Team of the Year – which club were they playing for at the time?

1 TAMMY ABRAHAM

LEEDS ☐
ASTON VILLA ☐
CHARLTON ☐

2 JAMES MADDISON

NORWICH ☐
LEICESTER ☐
BRISTOL CITY ☐

3 CHRIS WOOD

LEEDS ☐
IPSWICH ☐
MILWALL ☐

4 RYAN SESSEGNON

BRENTFORD ☐
DERBY ☐
FULHAM ☐

5 DEAN HENDERSON

SHREWSBURY ☐
DONCASTER ☐
SHEFFIELD UNITED ☐

6 HARRY MAGUIRE

HULL ☐
SHEFFIELD UNITED ☐
BOLTON ☐

7 DELE ALLI

MK DONS ☐
LUTON ☐
STEVENAGE ☐

8 KIERAN TRIPPIER

BURNLEY ☐
ROTHERHAM ☐
BLACKPOOL ☐

9 CALLUM WILSON

COVENTRY ☐
NOTTINGHAM FOREST ☐
CARDIFF ☐

ANSWERS ON P153   **MY SCORE** ☐ /9

FOOTBALL LEAGUE LEGENDS!

Q These old-school stars were all named in a PFA Football League Team of the Year – which club were they playing for?

1 DENIS IRWIN

LEEDS	
OLDHAM	
SHEFFIELD WEDNESDAY	

2 GORDON STRACHAN

SOUTHAMPTON	
LEEDS	
SUNDERLAND	

3 STEVE BULL

COVENTRY	
WOLVES	
BIRMINGHAM	

4 DANNY MURPHY

FULHAM	
CREWE	
MILLWALL	

5 JOHN McGINLAY

BOLTON	
STOKE	
IPSWICH	

6 ROBERT PROSINECKI

DERBY	
PORTSMOUTH	
WEST HAM	

7 SAM ALLARDYCE

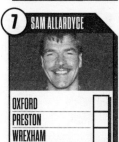

OXFORD	
PRESTON	
WREXHAM	

8 TONY CASCARINO

LEICESTER	
GILLINGHAM	
HUDDERSFIELD	

9 DAVID JAMES

WATFORD	
WIMBLEDON	
WALSALL	

ANSWERS ON P153 **MY SCORE** /9

STADIUM NAME GAME!

Q Can you name the stadium where these Football League clubs play home games?

1

OAKWELL
ABBEY STADIUM
BRUNTON PARK

2

THE HAWTHORNS
ST ANDREW'S
MADEJSKI STADIUM

3

ASHTON GATE
MEMORIAL STADIUM
KENILWORTH ROAD

4

DEEPDALE
DW STADIUM
PRIDE PARK

5

HILLSBOROUGH STADIUM
KCOM STADIUM
CRAVEN COTTAGE

6

KIRKLEES STADIUM
SIXFIELDS STADIUM
BRISBANE ROAD

7

BOUNDARY PARK
EWOOD PARK
HOME PARK

8

PORTMAN ROAD
THE DEN
LIBERTY STADIUM

9

FRATTON PARK
ADAMS PARK
BLOOMFIELD ROAD

ANSWERS ON P153   **MY SCORE** [   ] **/9**

STADIUM
NAME GAME!

Q Can you name the stadium where these Football League clubs play home games?

1

HIGHBURY STADIUM ☐
MOSS ROSE ☐
PIRELLI STADIUM ☐

2

GLANFORD PARK ☐
PRENTON PARK ☐
GLOBE ARENA ☐

3

KENILWORTH ROAD ☐
PRIESTFIELD STADIUM ☐
BESCOT STADIUM ☐

4

RACECOURSE GROUND ☐
FIELD MILL ☐
KEEPMOAT STADIUM ☐

5

MEADOW LANE ☐
ROOTS HALL ☐
VICTORIA ROAD ☐

6

SINCIL BANK ☐
PLAINMOOR ☐
CITY GROUND ☐

7

VALLEY PARADE ☐
THE VALLEY ☐
RODNEY PARADE ☐

8

BRUNTON PARK ☐
BLUNDELL PARK ☐
PRENTON PARK ☐

9

SPOTLAND STADIUM ☐
BOUNDARY PARK ☐
THE SHAY ☐

ANSWERS ON P153 **MY SCORE** ☐ **/9**

WOMEN'S FOOTBALL

Almost three decades after the first Women's World Cup and a whopping 128 years since the first women's match in the UK – women's footy has exploded onto the global stage! But how much do you know about the superstars of the WSL and international game? Ready, set, go quizzers!

WOMEN'S FOOTY
GUESS WHO?

Q These ballers all played in the 2019-20 WSL season – but can you put names to the faces?

1

GABRIELLE GEORGE
CHLOE KELLY
SIMONE MAGILL

2

LAUREN JAMES
ABBIE MCMANUS
JESS SIGSWORTH

3

GEMMA BONNER
STEPH HOUGHTON
ELLEN WHITE

4

RAMONA BACHMANN
BETH ENGLAND
GURO REITEN

5

VIVIANNE MIEDEMA
JORDAN NOBBS
DANIELLE VAN DE DONK

6

AMALIE EIKELAND
NATASHA HARDING
FARA WILLIAMS

7

AOIFE MANNION
ELLIE ROEBUCK
DEMI STOKES

8

GILLY FLAHERTY
LEANNE KIERNAN
ALISHA LEHMANN

9

JENNIFER BEATTIE
KIM LITTLE
LEAH WILLIAMSON

ANSWERS ON P153 **MY SCORE** [ ] /9

WOMEN'S FOOTY

GUESS WHO?

1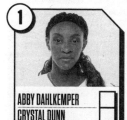

ABBY DAHLKEMPER
CRYSTAL DUNN
JESSICA MCDONALD

2

CAITLIN FOORD
SAM KERR
CHLOE LOGARZO

3

CRISTIANE
FORMIGA
MARTA

4

JANINE BECKIE
ADRIANA LEON
CHRISTINE SINCLAIR

5

KAREN BARDSLEY
MARY EARPS
CARLY TELFORD

6

AMANDINE HENRY
GAETANE THINEY
EUGENIE LE SOMMER

7

SARA DABRITZ
LEONIE MAIER
ALEXANDRA POPP

8

STINA BLACKSTENIUS
HEDVIG LINDAHL
FRIDOLINA ROLFO

9

JACKIE GROENEN
LIEKE MARTENS
SARI VAN VEENENDAAL

ANSWERS ON P153   **MY SCORE** [   ] /9

WOMEN'S BALLER
L I N E - U P S !

1

ROEBUCK

BECKIE HOUGHTON · BONNER STOKES

WALSH   WEIR

SCOTT   HEMP

STANWAY   WHITE

2

BERGER

MJELDE BRIGHT · ERIKSSON ANDERSSON

CUTHBERT   INGLE   REITEN

JI

KERR · ENGLAND

3

PEYRAUD-MAGNIN

WILLIAMSON SCHNADERBECK

MAIER   McCABE

LITTLE   WALTI

EVANS   NOBBS · VAN DE DONK

MIEDEMA

4

EARPS

HARRIS A. TURNER · M. TURNER SMITH

GROENEN   LADD   ZELEM

ROSS   SIGSWORTH   JAMES

ANSWERS ON P153   **MY SCORE**   /4

WOMEN'S BALLER
L I N E - U P S !

Q Can you name these 2020 SheBelieves Cup countries below?

1

NAEHER

DAHLKEMPER · SAUERBRUNN

O'HARA · DUNN

LAVELLE — ERTZ — HORAN

HEATH · LLOYD · PRESS

....

2

PANOS

MORAZA · PEREIRA — LEON · OUAHABI

GUIJARRO — BONMATI · SOSA

SAMPEDRO · CALDENTEY

GARCIA

....

3

IKEDA

SHIMIZI · DOKO — MIYAKE · MIYAGAWA

MOMIKI · SUGITA — MIURA · NAKAJIMA

IWABUCHI

TANAKA

....

4

ROEBUCK

DALY · HOUGHTON · BRIGHT · STOKES

WALSH

KELLY · NOBBS · STANWAY · HEMP

ENGLAND

....

PREMIER LEAGUE

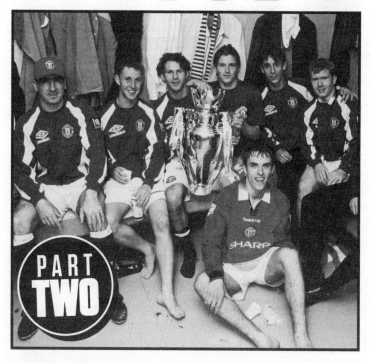

PART TWO

It's time for another instalment of quiz action focused on the top flight of English footy. We're talking about the modern-day heroes, superstars of yesteryear and legendary teams from the Premier League era. Who will ace this round? Let's go, quizzers!

PLAYER OF THE YEAR

PUZZLER!

Q Here are the PFA Player of the Year winners from the last ten seasons of the Premier League – can you fill in the blanks?

SEASON	PLAYER OF THE YEAR	CLUB	
2009-10	W R	MAN. UNITED	
2010-11	G B	TOTTENHAM	
2011-12	ROBIN VAN PERSIE		
2012-13	GARETH BALE		
2013-14	L S	LIVERPOOL	
2014-15	E H	CHELSEA	
2015-16	RIYAD MAHREZ		
2016-17	N K	CHELSEA	
2017-18	M S	LIVERPOOL	
2018-19	V V	LIVERPOOL	

ANSWERS ON P153   **MY SCORE** ☐ **/10**

PLAYER OF THE YEAR

PUZZLER!

Q Here are the PFA Player of the Year winners from the first ten seasons of the Premier League – can you fill in the blanks?

SEASON	PLAYER OF THE YEAR	CLUB	
1992-93	PAUL McGRATH		
1993-94	E C	MAN. UNITED	
1994-95	ALAN SHEARER		
1995-96	LES FERDINAND		
1996-97	ALAN SHEARER		
1997-98	D B	ARSENAL	
1998-99	D G	TOTTENHAM	
1999-2000	R K	MAN. UNITED	
2000-01	T S	MAN. UNITED	
2001-02	R V	MAN. UNITED	

ANSWERS ON P153   **MY SCORE** ☐ /10

START•STOP
01:00
MIN   SEC

Q You've got 60 seconds to answer as many of these questions below as possible!

1 Which club did forward Mohamed Salah play for before joining Liverpool?

....

2 In which stadium do Crystal Palace play their Premier League home games?

....

3 Which country does Leicester right-back Ricardo Pereira play for?

....

4 Can you name the German manager of East Anglian club Norwich?

....

5 Which is the biggest stadium in the Premier League?

....

6 Which Premier League club is nicknamed The Blades?

....

7 Which Bundesliga club did Christian Pulisic leave to join Chelsea in 2019?

....

8 Who was manager of Man. United the last time they won the Premier League?

....

9 Who was the last English player to be named PFA Player of the Year?

....

10 Mikel Arteta was assistant manager at which top club before taking charge at Arsenal?

....

ANSWERS ON P153   **MY SCORE** [   ] **/10**

BEAT THE CLOCK

START•STOP 01:00 MIN SEC

Q You've got 60 seconds to answer as many of these questions below as possible!

1 Croatian Alen Boksic played for which English club between 2000 and 2003?

....

2 Which Premier League club was managed by Brian Horton between 1993 and 1995?

....

3 Man. United won the first ever Premier League title in 1993 – but who finished second?

....

4 Mo Johnston and Tony Cottee were team-mates at which Prem club in the 1990s?

....

5 Who played at Highfield Road during their Prem days between 1992 and 2001?

....

6 Which club was Kevin Phillips playing for when he won the Prem Golden Boot?

....

7 Which Premier League club was sponsored by Dr Martens between 1998 and 2003?

....

8 World Cup-winning forward Christophe Dugarry played in the Prem for which club?

....

9 Which club did David Bardsley captain in the Prem during the 1993-94 season?

....

10 Which manager quit as Swindon boss in 1993 to take charge at Chelsea?

....

ANSWERS ON P153 **MY SCORE** ☐ **/10**

GENERAL KNOWLEDGE CROSSWORD!

Q Use the ten clues below to fill in this crossword – with a Premier League trivia theme!

ACROSS

2 Club in blue from the city of Liverpool (7)
4 Wolves star who joined from Atletico Madrid in 2017, Diogo _____ (4)
7 Man. United ace signed from Monaco in 2015, Anthony _____ (7)
8 The manager of Sheffield United (5,6)
9 Man. City centre-back born in Agen in France, _____ Laporte (7)
10 The Clarets from Turf Moor (7)

DOWN

1 Leicester midfielder Wilfred Ndidi plays for this country (7)
3 The club that plays at the Vitality Stadium (11)
5 Arsenal's home before their move to the Emirates in 2006 (8)
6 Scottish boss who's managed Everton, Man. United and West Ham (5,5)

ANSWERS ON P153   **MY SCORE** [ ] /10

GENERAL KNOWLEDGE CROSSWORD!

Q Use the ten clues below to fill in this crossword – theme is Prem trivia from back in the day!

ACROSS

3 Speedy winger for Norwich, Newcastle and Tottenham in the 1990s (4,3)
7 Liverpool's record signing when he joined from Leicester in 2000 (5,6)
8 Peter Ndlovu played 154 games for this club between 1991 and 1997 (8)
9 Captain of Blackburn's title-winning team, Tim _____ (8)
10 Dutch winger at Nottingham Forest in the mid 1990s, Brian ___ (3)

DOWN

1 Utility player for Sheffield Wednesday and Blackburn, Paul _____ (8)
2 The club that played at The Dell until 2001 (11)
4 German striker at Man. City between 1994 and 1998 (3,6)
5 Ex-QPR and Tottenham manager, Gerry _____ (7)
6 Man. United's kit sponsor from 1982 to 2000 (5)

2019-20
LINE-UPS!

Q Which Premier League clubs lined up with these players during the 2019-20 season?

1

RYAN

MONTOYA WEBSTER DUNK BURN

GROSS PROPPER STEPHENS MOOY

CONNOLLY MAUPAY

....

2

HEATON

GUILBERT ENGELS MINGS TARGETT

McGINN NAKAMBA LUIZ

EL GHAZI WESLEY GREALISH

....

3

HENDERSON

BASHAM EGAN O'CONNELL

BALDOCK LUNDSTRAM NORWOOD FLECK STEVENS

McBURNIE MOUSSET

....

4

DUBRAVKA

FERNANDEZ LASCELLES SCHAR

LAZARO ROSE

LONGSTAFF - BENTALEB

ALMIRON SAINT-MAXIMIN

JOELINTON

....

ANSWERS ON P153 **MY SCORE** ☐ /4

LEGENDARY
LINE-UPS!

Q Which Premier League clubs lined up with these players during the competition's history?

1

SCHWARZER

FESTA · PALLISTER · VICKERS

COOPER · GORDON

GASCOIGNE · TOWNSEND · MUSTOE

BECK · RICARD

2

JAASKALAINEN

MENDY · N'GOTTY · BERGSSON · CHARLTON

FRANDSEN · CAMPO · OKOCHA · GARDNER

DJORKAEFF · PEDERSEN

3

SIMONSEN

HIBBERT · WEIR · STUBBS · UNSWORTH

ALEXANDERSSON · GRAVESEN · LI TIE · NAYSMITH

CAMPBELL · RADZINSKI

4

HOULT

SCHNOOR · PRIOR · STIMAC · LAURSEN

DELAP · CARSLEY · POWELL · BOHINEN

WANCHOPE · STURRIDGE

IT'S A TEAM GAME!

Q These nine ballers all appeared in the Premier League in recent years – but can you remember which club they played for?

1 STEVEN DEFOUR

HUDDERSFIELD
BURNLEY
SHEFFIELD UNITED

2 JOEL CAMPBELL

LEICESTER
ARSENAL
WATFORD

3 CHRISTIAN POULSEN

LIVERPOOL
TOTTENHAM
WEST HAM

4 YOAN GOUFFRAN

LEICESTER
NEWCASTLE
CRYSTAL PALACE

5 JORDY CLASIE

SOUTHAMPTON
SHEFFIELD UNITED
WOLVES

6 VLAD CHIRICHES

TOTTENHAM
ASTON VILLA
BOURNEMOUTH

7 JESUS NAVAS
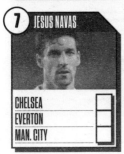
CHELSEA
EVERTON
MAN. CITY

8 SHINJI KAGAWA

MAN. UNITED
SOUTHAMPTON
ARSENAL

9 ALEXANDRE PATO

WOLVES
CHELSEA
WATFORD

ANSWERS ON P153   **MY SCORE** ☐ **/9**

IT'S A **TEAM GAME!**

Q These nine ballers all appeared in the Premier League back in the day – but can you remember which club they played for?

1 COBI JONES

SHEFFIELD WEDNESDAY
BLACKBURN
COVENTRY

2 DMITRI KHARINE

QPR
CHELSEA
EVERTON

3 GHEORGHE POPESCU

WEST HAM
TOTTENHAM
CHELSEA

4 PAULO FUTRE

WEST HAM
SOUTHAMPTON
IPSWICH

5 REGI BLINKER

CHARLTON
SHEFFIELD WEDNESDAY
LEEDS

6 ALJOSA ASANOVIC

DERBY
NOTTINGHAM FOREST
EVERTON

7 CLARENCE ACUNA

NEWCASTLE
SUNDERLAND
MIDDLESBROUGH

8 YOUSSEF CHIPPO

COVENTRY
ASTON VILLA
LEICESTER

9 DANIEL AMOKACHI

NORWICH
EVERTON
NEWCASTLE

ANSWERS ON P153 **MY SCORE** /9

TITLE WINNERS

WORDSEARCH!

> **Q** Only SEVEN clubs have won the Premier League since its creation in 1992 – can you find them all in the grid below?

A	C	B	S	R	X	Y	V	M	N	B	M
E	U	G	B	W	Z	Q	E	J	Y	D	A
S	S	U	K	H	Y	T	A	V	R	B	N
L	L	T	F	C	U	K	Q	C	A	D	U
E	E	U	A	Y	T	I	C	N	A	M	N
H	I	A	I	A	R	S	E	N	A	L	I
C	C	V	L	U	T	L	E	G	M	W	T
Z	E	B	L	A	C	K	B	U	R	N	E
D	S	P	S	S	H	R	O	F	W	B	D
I	T	I	K	D	T	H	L	X	E	B	E
N	E	W	L	O	O	P	R	E	V	I	L
S	R	O	R	W	R	I	N	G	W	V	Z

ANSWERS ON P153   **MY SCORE** ☐ **/7**

TITLE WINNERS

W O R D S E A R C H !

Q We've hidden the surnames of SEVEN managers who have led clubs to the Prem title in the grid below – can you find them?

C	I	R	W	E	N	G	E	R	N	F	E
U	T	N	A	W	R	S	F	O	E	T	N
I	T	D	I	H	K	X	S	Q	N	G	Z
P	O	H	A	R	N	U	G	O	L	M	B
O	L	X	J	L	G	R	C	M	J	I	A
O	E	A	X	R	G	E	W	N	B	T	N
L	C	L	E	V	H	L	L	M	Z	F	N
L	N	F	P	N	G	N	I	L	H	R	E
H	A	E	I	Y	S	Q	I	S	E	E	R
M	O	U	R	I	N	H	O	K	H	P	O
I	N	O	D	N	A	A	I	Z	F	R	W
P	X	F	A	L	O	I	D	R	A	U	G

INTERNATIONAL FOOTBALL

It's time to turn our attention to the international game once again – to look at the legends who have written their names into the history books and the heroes who have become national icons. If you've got what it takes, turn the page now and get stuck in, quizzers!

BADGE
BAMBOOZLER!

Q Can you tell us which countries have these crests on their shirts?

1

BELGIUM
SPAIN
PORTUGAL

2

SWEDEN
COLOMBIA
BRAZIL

3

HOLLAND
KOSOVO
SOUTH KOREA

4

CHINA
WALES
NORTH KOREA

5

GIBRALTAR
PARAGUAY
PORTUGAL

6

AUSTRALIA
ARGENTINA
FRANCE

7

GERMANY
DENMARK
RUSSIA

8

ARGENTINA
AUSTRALIA
URUGUAY

9

SERBIA
CROATIA
CZECH REPUBLIC

ANSWERS ON P153   **MY SCORE**   /9

BADGE BAMBOOZLER!

Q Can you tell us which countries have these crests on their shirts?

1

DENMARK ☐
BELGIUM ☐
BOLIVIA ☐

2

KENYA ☐
SOUTH AFRICA ☐
ZAMBIA ☐

3

FINLAND ☐
SAN MARINO ☐
SWEDEN ☐

4

POLAND ☐
PARAGUAY ☐
PERU ☐

5
ALGERIA ☐
LIBYA ☐
QATAR ☐

6

MOROCCO ☐
TURKEY ☐
TUNISIA ☐

7

RUSSIA ☐
HUNGARY ☐
CZECH REPUBLIC ☐

8

ALBANIA ☐
AUSTRIA ☐
POLAND ☐

9

IVORY COAST ☐
CAMEROON ☐
GABON ☐

NATIONAL HEROES!

Q These players are the all-time top scorers for their country – but which country?

1 PELE

- BRAZIL
- ARGENTINA
- ITALY

2 ZLATAN IBRAHIMOVIC

- SWEDEN
- DENMARK
- SERBIA

3 DAVID VILLA

- PORTUGAL
- ITALY
- SPAIN

4 EDIN DZEKO

- SERBIA
- BOSINA & HERZEGOVINA
- ALBANIA

5 RADAMAEL FALCAO

- ECUADOR
- COLOMBIA
- CHILE

6 SALOMON RONDON

- VENEZUELA
- PERU
- COSTA RICA

7 MAREK HAMSIK

- SLOVAKIA
- SLOVENIA
- ROMANIA

8 ANDRIY SHEVCHENKO

- RUSSIA
- UKRAINE
- BELARUS

9 SAMUEL ETO'O

- IVORY COAST
- CAMEROON
- MALI

ANSWERS ON P153   **MY SCORE** /9

NATIONAL HEROES!

Q These players are the all-time top scorers for their country – but which country?

1 ALI DAEI

IRAN	
IRAQ	
SAUDI ARABIA	

2 JAN KOLLER

CZECH REPUBLIC	
ROMANIA	
POLAND	

3 SHAUN GOATER

BAHAMAS	
BENIN	
BERMUDA	

4 GEORGE WEAH

DR CONGO	
SIERRA LEONE	
LIBERIA	

5 STEPHANE SESSEGNON

SURINAME	
MALI	
BENIN	

6 RASHIDI YEKINI

CAMEROON	
GABON	
NIGERIA	

7 STERN JOHN

JAMAICA	
GRENADA	
TRINIDAD & TOBAGO	

8 FERENC PUSKAS

HUNGARY	
AUSTRIA	
BULGARIA	

9 ASAMOAH GYAN

SENEGAL	
GHANA	
IVORY COAST	

ENGLAND

MISSING STARS

Q Using their initials, can you identify the England players in the line-ups from these classic matches?

1 2018 World Cup semi-final

CROATIA 2-1 **ENGLAND**

A	
B	
C	
D	
E	
F	
G	
H	
I	
J	
K	

2 Euro 2016 Group B match

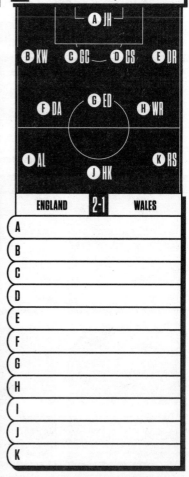

ENGLAND 2-1 **WALES**

A	
B	
C	
D	
E	
F	
G	
H	
I	
J	
K	

ANSWERS ON P153 **MY SCORE** /22

ENGLAND
MISSING STARS

Q Using their initials, can you identify the England players in the line-ups from these classic matches?

1 Euro 1996 semi-final

- **A** DS
- **B** GS
- **C** TA
- **D** SP
- **E** DA
- **F** PI
- **G** SM
- **H** DP
- **I** PG
- **J** TS
- **K** AS

GERMANY WON 6-5 ON PENALTIES

| GERMANY | 1-1 | ENGLAND |

A
B
C
D
E
F
G
H
I
J
K

2 1990 World Cup semi-final

- **A** PS
- **B** MW
- **C** PP
- **D** DW
- **E** TB
- **F** SP
- **G** DP
- **H** PG
- **I** CW
- **J** GL
- **K** PB

WEST GERMANY WON 6-5 ON PENALTIES

| WEST GERMANY | 1-1 | ENGLAND |

A
B
C
D
E
F
G
H
I
J
K

ANSWERS ON P153 **MY SCORE** ☐ **/22**

GENERAL KNOWLEDGE CROSSWORD!

Q Use our clues to fill the crossword – this one is about the international game. Good luck!

ACROSS

6 South American football tournament, _____ America (4)
7 Northern Ireland's home stadium in Belfast, _____ Park (7)
8 Captain of 2019 Africa Cup of Nations winners Algeria (5,6)
9 The current manager of Wales (4,5)
10 Top scorer at Euro 2016, Antoine _____ (9)

DOWN

1 The name given to fans of Scotland, _____ Army (6)
2 Winner of Euro 2016 and 2019 UEFA Nations League (8)
3 The national team of James Rodriguez (8)
4 Goalscoring wonderkid Erling Haaland plays for this country (6)
5 England manager between 2012 and 2016 (3,7)

ANSWERS ON P153 **MY SCORE** /10

GENERAL KNOWLEDGE CROSSWORD!

Q Use our clues to fill the crossword – this one is about the international game. Good luck!

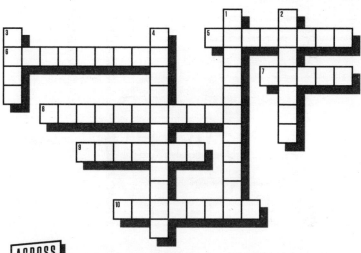

ACROSS

5 Czech Republic's most capped outfield player, Karel _ _ _ _ _ _ _ _ (8)
6 Legendary Belgian midfielder from the 1980s and 1990s (4,5)
7 Mark Pembridge, Paul Bodin and Eric Young played for this country (5)
8 Euro 96 Golden Boot winner (4,7)
9 The surprise winners of Euro 92 (7)
10 Country managed by Berti Vogts from 2002 to 2004 (8)

DOWN

1 Manager of England at Euro 88 (5,6)
2 Middle name of Argentina's legendary No.10, Diego _ _ _ _ _ _ _ Maradona (7)
3 The man born as Edson Arantes Do Nascimento (4)
4 Eccentric Mexico keeper from the 1990s (5,6)

FA CUP

The FA Cup – or the Football Association Challenge Cup, to give it its full name – is the world's oldest national cup competition. It's given us magical moments, unforgettable giant-killings and phenomenal finals over the past 148 years. Who'll claim cup glory here? Let's see, quizzers!

FA CUP FINAL
FLASHBACK!

Q In which years were these fantastic FA Cup final photos taken?

1

2018 ☐ 2019 ☐ 2017 ☐

2

2016 ☐ 2018 ☐ 2019 ☐

3

2015 ☐ 2016 ☐ 2017 ☐

4

2011 ☐ 2013 ☐ 2014 ☐

5

2012 ☐ 2013 ☐ 2014 ☐

6

2017 ☐ 2018 ☐ 2019 ☐

ANSWERS ON P153   **MY SCORE** ☐ **/6**

FA CUP FINAL
FLASHBACK!

Q In which years were these fantastic FA Cup final photos taken?

1

1994 ☐ 1996 ☐ 1998 ☐

2

1989 ☐ 1990 ☐ 1991 ☐

3

2003 ☐ 2006 ☐ 2009 ☐

4

2000 ☐ 2001 ☐ 2002 ☐

5

2004 ☐ 2005 ☐ 2006 ☐

6

1986 ☐ 1987 ☐ 1988 ☐

ANSWERS ON P153 **MY SCORE** ☐ /6

CUP FINAL GAFFERS!

Q Can you match the boss with the club he managed in an FA Cup final from 2012 to 2019?

1 PEP GUARDIOLA

2 ANTONIO CONTE

3 ARSENE WENGER

4 LOUIS VAN GAAL

5 KENNY DALGLISH

6 STEVE BRUCE

7 TIM SHERWOOD

8 ALAN PARDEW

9 ROBERTO MARTINEZ

10 JAVI GRACIA

A HULL

B ASTON VILLA

C CHELSEA

D ARSENAL

E WIGAN

F WATFORD

G MAN. CITY

H LIVERPOOL

I CRYSTAL PALACE

J MAN. UNITED

ANSWERS ON P153 **MY SCORE** /10

CUP FINAL GAFFERS!

Q Can you match the boss with the club he managed in an old-school FA Cup final?

1 JOE ROYLE

2 RUUD GULLIT

3 RAFAEL BENITEZ

4 BOBBY GOULD

5 JOHN SILLETT

6 TERRY VENABLES

7 RON ATKINSON

8 BOBBY ROBSON

9 JOHN LYALL

10 LAWRIE McMENEMY

A WIMBLEDON

B COVENTRY

C TOTTENHAM

D CHELSEA

E EVERTON

F IPSWICH

G LIVERPOOL

H MAN. UNITED

I SOUTHAMPTON

J WEST HAM

CUP FINAL
MISSING MEN

Q Can you name the missing stars from these FA Cup-winning teams?

1 2018-19

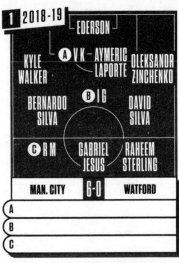

EDERSON

KYLE WALKER — **A** V K — AYMERIC LAPORTE — OLEKSANDR ZINCHENKO

BERNARDO SILVA — **B** I G — DAVID SILVA

C R M — GABRIEL JESUS — RAHEEM STERLING

| MAN. CITY | 6-0 | WATFORD |

A
B
C

2 2017-18

A T C

CESAR AZPILICUETA — GARY CAHILL — ANTONIO RUDIGER

TIEMOUE BAKAYOKO — N'GOLO KANTE — **B** C F — MARCOS ALONSO

C V M

OLIVIER GIROUD — EDEN HAZARD

| CHELSEA | 1-0 | MAN. UNITED |

A
B
C

3 2016-17

A D O

ROB HOLDING — **B** P M — NACHO MONREAL

AARON RAMSEY — GRANIT XHAKA

HECTOR BELLERIN — A. OXLADE-CHAMBERLAIN

MESUT OZIL — **C** D W — ALEXIS SANCHEZ

| ARSENAL | 2-1 | CHELSEA |

A
B
C

4 2015-16

DAVID DE GEA

ANTONIO VALENCIA — CHRIS SMALLING — **A** D B — MARCOS ROJO

B M C — **C** W R

JUAN MATA — MAROUANE FELLAINI — ANTHONY MARTIAL

MARCUS RASHFORD

| CRYSTAL PALACE | 1-2 | MAN. UNITED |

A
B
C

ANSWERS ON P153 — **MY SCORE** — /12

ADULT

CUP FINAL
MISSING MEN

Q Can you name the missing stars from these FA Cup-winning teams?

1 1993-94

PETER SCHMEICHEL

Ⓐ PP · STEVE BRUCE · GARY PALLISTER · DENIS IRWIN

Ⓑ AK · PAUL INCE · ROY KEANE · RYAN GIGGS

Ⓒ MH · ERIC CANTONA

| CHELSEA | 0-4 | MAN. UNITED |

A ___
B ___
C ___

2 1987-88

DAVE BEASANT

CLIVE GOODYEAR · ERIC YOUNG · ANDY THORN · TERRY PHELAN

ALAN CORK · Ⓐ LS · Ⓑ VJ · DENNIS WISE

TERRY GIBSON · Ⓒ JF

| LIVERPOOL | 0-1 | WIMBLEDON |

A ___
B ___
C ___

3 1990-91

ERIK THORSTVEDT

PAT VAN DEN HAUWE · STEVE SEDGLEY · GARY MABBUTT · JUSTIN EDINBURGH

Ⓐ PS · DAVID HOWELLS · Ⓑ PG

PAUL ALLEN · VINNY SAMWAYS

Ⓒ GL

| NOTT'M. FOREST | 1-2 | TOTTENHAM |

A ___
B ___
C ___

4 1992-93

DAVID SEAMAN

LEE DIXON · ANDY LINIGHAN · TONY ADAMS · Ⓐ NW

PAUL DAVIS · Ⓑ JJ · PAUL MERSON

Ⓒ KC · IAN WRIGHT · ALAN SMITH

| ARSENAL | 2-1 | SHEFFIELD WED. |

A ___
B ___
C ___

ANSWERS ON P153 **MY SCORE** ___ /12

motdmag.com **103**

SCOTTISH FOOTBALL

Two clubs have dominated Scottish football since the league was founded back in 1890 – Glasgow city rivals Celtic and Rangers. These two have gobbled up title after title – let's see how much you know about them and their Scottish Premiership challengers, quizzers!

BADGE
BAMBOOZLER!

Q Reckon you know which Scottish clubs these nine badges belong to?

1

ROSS COUNTY
RANGERS
RAITH ROVERS

2

ALLOA
CELTIC
LIVINGSTON

3

CELTIC
HIBERNIAN
ROSS COUNTY

4

ABERDEEN
HAMILTON
DUNDEE

5

DUNFERMLINE
EAST FIFE
MOTHERWELL

6

HAMILTON
HEARTS
MOTHERWELL

7

ROSS COUNTY
INVERNESS CT
KILMARNOCK

8

FALKIRK
DUNFERMLINE
ST MIRREN

9

DUNDEE UNITED
ABERDEEN
EAST FIFE

ANSWERS ON P153   **MY SCORE**   /9

OLD FIRM
T E A S E R !

Q These footy legends played for either Rangers or Celtic – do you know which?

1 MARK HATELEY

CELTIC
RANGERS

2 JORGE CADETE

CELTIC
RANGERS

3 STUART McCALL

CELTIC
RANGERS

4 LUBO MORAVCIK

CELTIC
RANGERS

5 JORG ALBERTZ

CELTIC
RANGERS

6 MORTEN WIEGHORST

CELTIC
RANGERS

7 S. NAKAMURA

CELTIC
RANGERS

8 LORENZO AMORUSO

CELTIC
RANGERS

9 MICHAEL MOLS
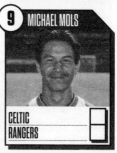
CELTIC
RANGERS

BEAT THE CLOCK!

START · STOP
01:00
MIN SEC

Q You've got 60 seconds to answer as many questions as you can on Scottish footy!

1 Which club has won the Scottish Premiership every year since 2012?

....

2 Which club is currently managed by ex-Scotland midfielder Derek McInnes?

....

3 Hibernian and which other Scottish Premiership club are based in Edinburgh?

....

4 Which legendary English midfielder is the current manager of Rangers?

....

5 Which stadium in the Scottish Premiership has the biggest capacity?

....

6 In which Scottish city are Premiership rivals Rangers and Celtic based?

....

7 Which Scottish Prem club plays its home games at Fir Park?

....

8 Scotland boss Steve Clarke quit which club to take charge of the national team?

....

9 Which Scottish club did Liverpool's Virgil van Dijk play for between 2013 and 2015?

....

10 The last time neither Rangers or Celtic won the league was in 1985 – who won it?

....

ANSWERS ON P153 **MY SCORE** /10

BEAT THE CLOCK!

START • STOP

01:00

MIN | SEC

Q You've got 60 seconds to answer as many questions as you can on Scottish footy!

1 Willie Miller played a record 797 games for which Scottish club?

....

2 Which Premiership club has been Scottish champions a record 54 times?

....

3 Scottish football legend Mixu Paatelainen played 70 times for which country?

....

4 Which iconic Danish winger left Rangers in 1998 to sign for Chelsea?

....

5 Which Scottish club lost to IFK Gothenburg in the 1987 UEFA Cup final?

....

6 Which Australian star won the Golden Boot in 2000 with 25 goals for Celtic?

....

7 Which striker scored 23 goals in his first ten games for Rangers in 1997?

....

8 Which club based in Perth play its home games at McDiarmid Park?

....

9 After scoring 242 goals in 313 games, Henrik Larsson left Celtic to join which club?

....

10 Which Scottish Prem club plays its home games at Easter Road?

....

ANSWERS ON P153 **MY SCORE** [ ] **/10**

LA LIGA/ SPAIN

Hola! We're now hopping over to Spain – home of sun, sea, sand and two genuine global superclubs. Real Madrid and Barcelona, two of the world's biggest teams, are football royalty – but how much do you know about them and their rivals from La Liga? Vamos, quizzers!

BARCA OR REAL?

1 RONALDO

BARCELONA ☐
REAL MADRID ☐
BOTH ☐

2 XABI ALONSO

BARCELONA ☐
REAL MADRID ☐
BOTH ☐

3 PEPE REINA

BARCELONA ☐
REAL MADRID ☐
BOTH ☐

4 RONALDINHO

BARCELONA ☐
REAL MADRID ☐
BOTH ☐

5 ANGEL DI MARIA

BARCELONA ☐
REAL MADRID ☐
BOTH ☐

6 THIERRY HENRY

BARCELONA ☐
REAL MADRID ☐
BOTH ☐

7 DIEGO MARADONA

BARCELONA ☐
REAL MADRID ☐
BOTH ☐

8 DAVID BECKHAM

BARCELONA ☐
REAL MADRID ☐
BOTH ☐

9 ARJEN ROBBEN

BARCELONA ☐
REAL MADRID ☐
BOTH ☐

ANSWERS ON P153 **MY SCORE** ☐ /9

REAL

OR
BARCA?

Q Here's a tough one – did these ledges play for Barcelona or Real Madrid, or both?

1 LUIS FIGO

BARCELONA ☐
REAL MADRID ☐
BOTH ☐

2 IVAN ZAMORANO

BARCELONA ☐
REAL MADRID ☐
BOTH ☐

3 LUDOVIC GIULY

BARCELONA ☐
REAL MADRID ☐
BOTH ☐

4 GHEORGE HAGI

BARCELONA ☐
REAL MADRID ☐
BOTH ☐

5 EMILIO BUTRAGUENO

BARCELONA ☐
REAL MADRID ☐
BOTH ☐

6 ROMARIO

BARCELONA ☐
REAL MADRID ☐
BOTH ☐

7 JULIO SALINAS

BARCELONA ☐
REAL MADRID ☐
BOTH ☐

8 MICHAEL LAUDRUP

BARCELONA ☐
REAL MADRID ☐
BOTH ☐

9 LUIS ENRIQUE

BARCELONA ☐
REAL MADRID ☐
BOTH ☐

ANSWERS ON P153   **MY SCORE** ☐ /9

BEAT THE CLOCK

START•STOP

01:00

MIN | **SEC**

Q You've got 60 seconds to answer as many La Liga questions as you can!

1 Barcelona striker Luis Suarez plays for which country?

....

2 What is the name of the current manager of Real Madrid?

....

3 Atletico Madrid signed wonderkid Joao Felix from which Portuguese club?

....

4 Which club was crowned La Liga champions in 2018-19?

....

5 Which player holds the record for the most hat-tricks in La Liga history?

....

6 Which Spanish club does striker Raul De Tomas play for?

....

7 La Liga legend Andres Iniesta left Barcelona to play in which country?

....

8 In which stadium do Valencia play their home games?

....

9 How many games did Spanish legend Raul play for Real Madrid – 550 or 660?

....

10 Which La Liga club has the nickname The Yellow Submarine?

....

ANSWERS ON P153 **MY SCORE** **/10**

BEAT THE CLOCK

START•STOP
01:00
MIN SEC

Q You've got 60 seconds to answer as many La Liga questions as you can!

1 Celta Vigo striker Iago Aspas once played for which Premier League club?

2 Which La Liga club did Gary Lineker play for between 1986 and 1989?

3 Which award did Atletico Madrid legend Diego Forlan win at the 2010 World Cup?

4 La Liga legend Xavi is now managing a club in which country?

5 Who was in goal for Real Madrid when they won the Champions League in 2013-14?

6 Which country did Barcelona centre-back Fernando Couto play for?

7 Which current La Liga 2 club lifted the top division title back in 1999-2000?

8 Which club took keeper Thibaut Courtois on loan from Chelsea from 2011 to 2014?

9 Which La Liga club did ex-Tottenham manager Mauricio Pochettino play for?

10 Which Italian club did Zinedine Zidane leave to join Real Madrid in 2001?

ANSWERS ON P153 **MY SCORE** /10

LEAGUE OF NATIONS!

Q Can you tell us which international teams these top-class La Liga ballers play for?

1 IVAN RAKITIC

CROATIA
HUNGARY
ROMANIA

2 GARETH BALE

ENGLAND
SCOTLAND
WALES

3 JAN OBLAK

SLOVAKIA
SLOVENIA
UKRAINE

4 EVER BANEGA

ARGENTINA
BOLIVIA
PERU

5 ALEXANDER ISAK

ICELAND
NORWAY
SWEDEN

6 ALLAN NYOM

CAMEROON
KENYA
ZAMBIA

7 DANIEL WASS

DENMARK
GERMANY
POLAND

8 SAMUEL CHUKWUEZE

ANGOLA
GHANA
NIGERIA

9 MAXIME GONALONS

BELGIUM
FRANCE
PORTUGAL

ANSWERS ON P153   **MY SCORE**   /9

LEAGUE OF NATIONS!

Q Can you remember which international teams these La Liga legends and cult heroes played for?

1 WALTER PANDIANI

CHILE
PARAGUAY
URUGUAY

2 FABIO CANNAVARO

AUSTRIA
ITALY
GREECE

3 JARI LITMANEN

ESTONIA
FINLAND
RUSSIA

4 FINIDI GEORGE

IVORY COAST
NIGERIA
SENEGAL

5 FREDDIE KANOUTE

BURUNDI
GUINEA
MALI

6 ROY MAKAAY

CZECH REPUBLIC
HOLLAND
SERBIA

7 PABLO AIMAR

ARGENTINA
BRAZIL
COLOMBIA

8 BENNI McCARTHY
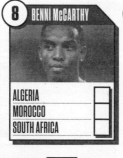
ALGERIA
MOROCCO
SOUTH AFRICA

9 HUGO SANCHEZ

CANADA
MEXICO
PANAMA

ANSWERS ON P153 **MY SCORE** /9

LA LIGA CROSSWORD!

Q Use the clues below to fill in the crossword – the theme is epic La Liga defenders!

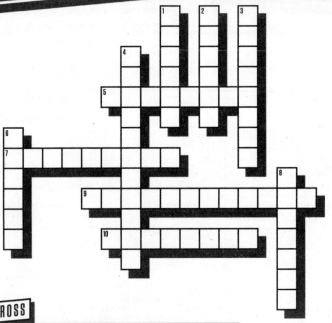

ACROSS

5 The nationality of Atletico Madrid full-back Sime Vrsaljko (8)
7 The club Alberto Moreno joined Villarreal from (9)
9 Nacho Monreal left Arsenal to join this club (4,8)
10 The tournament Samuel Umtiti won with France in 2018 (5,3)

DOWN

1 First name of English right-back, _____ Trippier (6)
2 The home country of iconic Real Madrid star Marcelo (6)
3 Eric Bailly's first club – it's either Espanyol or Mallorca (8)
4 Real Madrid's Panenka king and captain (6,5)
6 Second name of Villarreal's veteran centre-back, Raul _____ (6)
8 Valencia centre-back Eliaquim Mangala won the Prem with this club (3,4)

ANSWERS ON P153 **MY SCORE** /10

LA LIGA CROSSWORD!

Q Use the clues below to fill in the crossword – the theme is classic La Liga defenders!

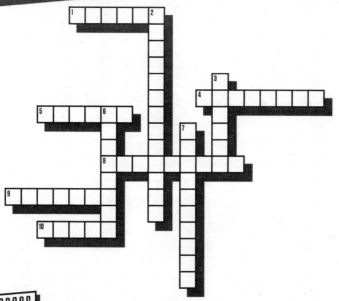

ACROSS

1 Ledge Valencia defender Miroslav Djukic is from this country (6)
4 Nationality of hard-as-nails Real Madrid defender, Pepe (8)
5 Surname of classic Barcelona right back, Albert _____ (6)
8 Country that Roberto Ayala played more than 100 games for (9)
9 Home nation of Atletico's title-winning captain, Diego Godin (7)
10 Barca's one-club man who won the 2008 Euros and 2010 World Cup, Carles _____ (5)

DOWN

2 Real Madrid full-back who briefly played for West Ham, initials AA (6,7)
3 Barca's goalscoring Dutch centre-back who managed Everton, Ronald _____ (6)
6 Club that Pablo Zabaleta left to join Man. City (8)
7 Italian club Real Madrid signed Roberto Carlos from (5,5)

ANSWERS ON P153 **MY SCORE** [ ] /10

LIGUE 1/ FRANCE

Bonjour! Oui oui, mon ami. It's time to wave goodbye to Spain as we arrive in neighbouring France. Ligue 1, the French top division, has produced some of the world's greatest footballing talents over the years – and it's currently home to PSG, a true European superpower. Have you got what it takes to conquer this round? Allez, quizzers!

PLAYER OF THE YEAR PUZZLER!

Q Below are the Ligue 1 Player of the Year winners from the last ten years – can you fill in the blanks?

SEASON	PLAYER OF THE YEAR	NATIONALITY	CLUB
2009-10	LISANDRO LOPEZ	_____	LYON
2010-11	_____	BELGIAN	LILLE
2011-12	EDEN HAZARD	BELGIAN	LILLE
2012-13	ZLATAN IBRAHIMOVIC	SWEDISH	PSG
2013-14	ZLATAN IBRAHIMOVIC	SWEDISH	PSG
2014-15	A_____ L_____	FRENCH	LYON
2015-16	ZLATAN IBRAHIMOVIC	SWEDISH	PSG
2016-17	EDINSON CAVANI	_____	PSG
2017-18	N_____	BRAZILIAN	PSG
2018-19	K____ M____	FRENCH	PSG

ANSWERS ON P153　**MY SCORE** ☐ /6

PLAYER OF THE YEAR PUZZLER!

SEASON	PLAYER OF THE YEAR	NATIONALITY	CLUB
1993-94	DAVID GINOLA	FRENCH	_____
1994-95	VINCENT GUERIN	FRENCH	PSG
1995-96	ZINEDINE ZIDANE	FRENCH	_____
1996-97	SONNY _____	BRAZILIAN	MONACO
1997-98	MARCO SIMONE	_____	PSG
1998-99	ALI _____	ALGERIAN	BORDEAUX
1999-2000	MARCELO GALLARDO	_____	MONACO
2000-01	ERIC CARRIERE	FRENCH	NANTES
2001-02	PAULETA	PORTUGUESE	BORDEAUX
2002-03	PAULETA	PORTUGUESE	BORDEAUX

ANSWERS ON P153   **MY SCORE** ⬜ /6

PSG PUZZLER CROSSWORD!

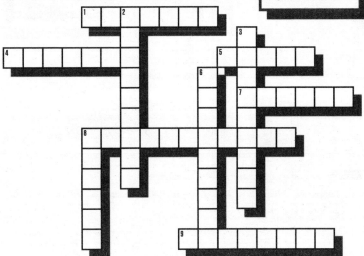

ACROSS

1 English legend who played for PSG in 2013, David _____ (7)
4 The home of PSG, Parc Des _____ (7)
5 PSG's owners are from this country (5)
7 The club's all-time record goalscorer, Edinson _____ (6)
8 Club captain and Brazil international (6,5)
9 Midfielder signed from Pescara in Serie A in 2012, Marco _____ (8)

DOWN

2 Country of PSG keeper Keylor Navas (5,4)
3 Neymar's club before his record £198m switch to Paris (9)
6 PSG'S opponent in the fiery match dubbed Le Classique (9)
8 Ex-Borussia Dortmund boss now in the PSG hotseat, Thomas _____ (6)

ANSWERS ON P153 **MY SCORE** ☐ /10

FRENCH FOOTY CROSSWORD!

Q Use the clues below to fill in the crossword – the theme is French footy!

ACROSS

1 The first club of ex-Arsenal winger Robert Pires (4)
4 Prolific striker Clive Allen quit Spurs to join this club in 1988 (8)
5 Five-time winner of the Ligue 1 Golden Boot, Jean-Pierre _____ (5)
6 English winger who won Ligue 1 three times with Marseille, Chris _____ (6)
7 French centre-back who left Strasbourg in 1996 to join Chelsea (5,7)
9 1998-99 Ligue 1 top scorer who joined Arsenal in 2000, Sylvain _____ (7)

DOWN

1 Glenn Hoddle and Mark Hateley played for this Ligue 1 club (6)
2 World Cup winner and ex-Monaco striker, David _____ (9)
3 Lyon's free-kick king from 2000 to 2009, _____ Pernambucano (7)
8 Ex-Brazil captain and PSG playmaker between 1993-98 (3)

BUNDESLIGA/ GERMANY

Buckle up as we travel to the Bundesliga – the German top-flight and one of the world's elite leagues. It's home to giants like Bayern Munich and Borussia Dortmund, and it attracts some of the biggest crowds in the whole of Europe. Will you be bamboozled by our brainteasers, quizzers?

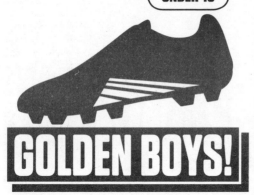

GOLDEN BOYS!

Q Here are the Bundesliga Golden Boot winners from the last ten years – can you fill in the blanks?

SEASON	TOP SCORER	CLUB	GOALS
2009-10	EDIN _____	WOLFSBURG	22
2010-11	MARIO GOMEZ	BAYERN MUNICH	28
2011-12	KLAAS-JAN _____	SCHALKE	29
2012-13	STEFAN KIESSLING	BAYER _____	25
2013-14	ROBERT LEWANDOWSKI	_____	20
2014-15	ALEXANDER MEIER	EINTRACHT FRANKFURT	19
2015-16	ROBERT LEWANDOWSKI	BAYERN MUNICH	30
2016-17	P. AUBAMEYANG	BORUSSIA DORTMUND	31
2017-18	ROBERT LEWANDOWSKI	BAYERN MUNICH	29
2017-18	ROBERT LEWANDOWSKI	BAYERN MUNICH	22

ANSWERS ON P153 **MY SCORE** [ ] /4

WHO AM I?

Q Here are four total Bundesliga legends – can you guess who they are from the clues?

PLAYER 1

- I was born in Dresden, in the old East Germany, in September 1967
- I became a star in the 1990s – during my time at Stuttgart, Inter Milan and Borussia Dortmund
- I was a defensive midfielder before switching to playing as a sweeper – a position in which I became the best in the world
- I won the Champions League and two Bundesliga titles with Dortmund
- I inspired Germany to victory at Euro '96, where I was named Player of the Tournament

PLAYER 2

- I was born in Erlangen, Germany, in March 1961
- I played for Borussia Monchengladbach, Bayern Munich and Inter Milan in the 1980s and 1990s
- I am regarded as one of the greatest midfielders of all time, known for my range of passing, driving runs and long-range shooting
- In 1990, I captained West Germany to victory at the World Cup and was also named European Footballer of the Year
- I played in five World Cups and got a record 150 Germany caps before retiring in 2000

PLAYER 3

- I was born in Londrina, Brazil, in July 1972
- I moved to Stuttgart in 1994 and signed for Bayern Munich three years later
- In six seasons at Bayern I scored 139 goals in 265 games – winning four Bundesliga titles and the Champions League
- I was a dynamic and explosive striker – finishing as the club's top scorer in all but one of my seasons in Munich
- I left Bayern in 2003 to sign for Lyon, then retired from football three years later

PLAYER 4

- I was born in Planaltina, Brazil, in May 1978
- In 2002, a year after signing for Bayer Leverkusen, I scored in the Champions League final against Real Madrid – but we lost 2-1
- After three seasons I moved to Bayern Munich, where I won three league titles and the German Cup three times
- I won the World Cup in 2002 with Brazil, as well as the Confederations Cup in 2005 and 2009
- I was a tall, strong centre-back known for my galloping runs out of defence

ANSWERS ON P153 **MY SCORE** ☐ /4

LEAGUE OF NATIONS!

Q These nine ballers are bossing it in the Bundesliga – but do you know which country they each play for?

1 ALPHONSO DAVIES

CANADA
MEXICO
USA

2 BREEL EMBOLO

SLOVAKIA
SLOVENIA
SWITZERLAND

3 MARCEL SABITZER

AUSTRIA
HUNGARY
ICELAND

4 ERLING HAALAND

DENMARK
FINLAND
NORWAY

5 LEON BAILEY

EL SALVADOR
JAMAICA
VENEZUELA

6 VINCENZO GRIFO

GREECE
ITALY
ROMANIA

7 KOEN CASTEELS

BELGIUM
PORTUGAL
SERBIA

8 IHLAS BEBOU

BENIN
GHANA
TOGO

9 BAS DOST

ANDORRA
FRANCE
HOLLAND

ANSWERS ON P153   **MY SCORE**   /9

LEAGUE OF NATIONS!

Q These nine players made their name in the Bundesliga – do you know which country they played for?

1 ARTHUR BOKA

ANGOLA
IVORY COAST
MOZAMBIQUE

2 DANIEL VAN BUYTEN

BELGIUM
FRANCE
SWEDEN

3 KRASIMIR BALAKOV

BULGARIA
MOLDOVA
UKRAINE

4 JUAN ARANGO

COLOMBIA
ECUADOR
VENEZUELA

5 JAY JAY OKOCHA

CAMEROON
NIGERIA
MOROCCO

6 IVICA OLIC

CROATIA
ESTONIA
LATVIA

7 STEVEN CHERUNDOLO

COSTA RICA
HONDURAS
USA

8 JAN POLAK

BELARUS
CZECH REPUBLIC
LITHUANIA

9 JOSHUA KENNEDY

AUSTRALIA
SOUTH KOREA
NEW ZEALAND

ANSWERS ON P153 **MY SCORE** ☐ /9

SERIE A/ ITALY

The final stop on our European tour is a visit to Italy – a country famous for glorious food, outstanding architecture and iconic football clubs. Serie A was the world's No.1 league back in the 1990s – but who'll be the No.1 in your house when it comes to Italian trivia? Smash it, quizzers!

BADGE
BAMBOOZLER!

1

INTER MILAN ☐
SAMPDORIA ☐
ATALANTA ☐

2

JUVENTUS ☐
TORINO ☐
INTER MILAN ☐

3

LECCE ☐
LAZIO ☐
PARMA ☐

4

NAPOLI ☐
CHIEVO ☐
INTER MILAN ☐

5

BOLOGNA ☐
AC MILAN ☐
TORINO ☐

6

ROMA ☐
BOLOGNA ☐
GENOA ☐

7

PARMA ☐
SAMPDORIA ☐
FIORENTINA ☐

8

ATALANTA ☐
FIORENTINA ☐
CAGLIARI ☐

9

GENOA ☐
BOLOGNA ☐
AC MILAN ☐

ANSWERS ON P153   **MY SCORE** ☐ /9

SERIE A RETRO STARS!

Q All you need to do is identify these nine Italian league legends and cult heroes – easy!

1

LUIS OLIVEIRA
EDMUNDO
ALDAIR

2

ANGELO DI LIVIO
GIANLUCA PESSOTTO
IGOR TUDOR

3

LILIAN THURAM
GEORGE WEAH
MARCEL DESAILLY

4

DEJAN STANKOVIC
SINISA MIHAJLOVIC
VLADIMIR JUGOVIC

5

ANTONIO BENARRIVO
ATTILIO LOMBARDO
NESTOR SENSINI

6

ALVARO RECOBA
DANIEL FONSECA
MARCELO SALAS

7

PAVEL NEDVED
MARCO DI VAIO
THOMAS DOLL

8

PAULO SOUSA
RUBEN SOSA
RUI COSTA

9

GIUSEPPE SIGNORI
MARCO DELVECCHIO
ENRICO CHIESA

CAREER PATH

Q See if you can name the four Juventus stars from their career history!

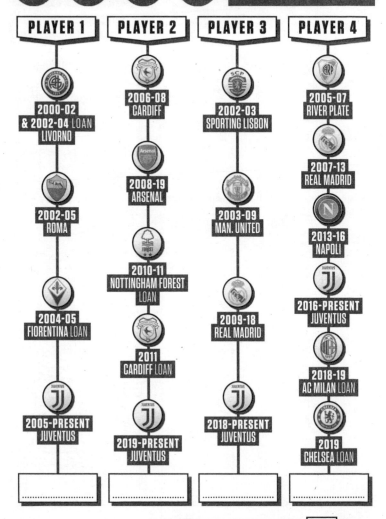

PLAYER 1

2000-02 & 2002-04 LOAN LIVORNO

2002-05 ROMA

2004-05 FIORENTINA LOAN

2005-PRESENT JUVENTUS

....

PLAYER 2

2006-08 CARDIFF

2008-19 ARSENAL

2010-11 NOTTINGHAM FOREST LOAN

2011 CARDIFF LOAN

2019-PRESENT JUVENTUS

....

PLAYER 3

2002-03 SPORTING LISBON

2003-09 MAN. UNITED

2009-18 REAL MADRID

2018-PRESENT JUVENTUS

....

PLAYER 4

2005-07 RIVER PLATE

2007-13 REAL MADRID

2013-16 NAPOLI

2016-PRESENT JUVENTUS

2018-19 AC MILAN LOAN

2019 CHELSEA LOAN

....

ANSWERS ON P153   **MY SCORE**   /4

CAREER PATH

Q Try to name the four Englishmen who spent time in Serie A from their career history!

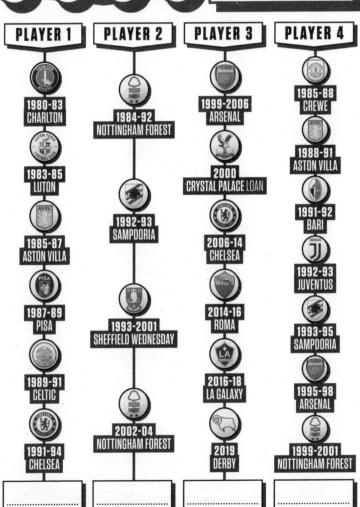

PLAYER 1	PLAYER 2	PLAYER 3	PLAYER 4
1980-83 CHARLTON	**1984-92** NOTTINGHAM FOREST	**1999-2006** ARSENAL	**1985-88** CREWE
1983-85 LUTON	**1992-93** SAMPDORIA	**2000** CRYSTAL PALACE LOAN	**1988-91** ASTON VILLA
1985-87 ASTON VILLA	**1993-2001** SHEFFIELD WEDNESDAY	**2006-14** CHELSEA	**1991-92** BARI
1987-89 PISA	**2002-04** NOTTINGHAM FOREST	**2014-16** ROMA	**1992-93** JUVENTUS
1989-91 CELTIC		**2016-18** LA GALAXY	**1993-95** SAMPDORIA
1991-94 CHELSEA		**2019** DERBY	**1995-98** ARSENAL
			1999-2001 NOTTINGHAM FOREST

GLOBAL GAME

You've tackled Europe's big leagues – now it's about to get trickier.
We're going on a whistle-stop tour of the world to put your knowledge
of the global game to the test. So grab your passport, quizzers, and join us
on an adventure to discover who's the real footy brainbox in your house!

COUNTRY CHALLENGE!

Q Can you match each European club with the country that it comes from?

1

HAJDUK SPLIT
CROATIA
SERBIA
AUSTRIA

2

BASEL
SWITZERLAND
AUSTRIA
GERMANY

3

VITESSE ARNHEM
POLAND
HOLLAND
FRANCE

4

ZENIT ST PETERSBURG
RUSSIA
UKRAINE
GEORGIA

5

BESIKTAS
GREECE
TURKEY
CZECH REPUBLIC

6

OLYMPIAKOS
ITALY
TURKEY
GREECE

7

SHAKHTAR DONETSK
RUSSIA
UKRAINE
SERBIA

8

EIBAR
SPAIN
PORTUGAL
FRANCE

9

SHAMROCK ROVERS
NORTHERN IRELAND
REPUBLIC OF IRELAND
WALES

ANSWERS ON P153 **MY SCORE** /9

COUNTRY CHALLENGE!

Q Can you match each European club with the country that it comes from?

1

BRONDBY
- SWEDEN
- DENMARK
- AUSTRIA

2

CLUJ
- BELARUS
- ROMANIA
- MOLDOVA

3

LUDOGORETS
- ALBANIA
- BULGARIA
- LITHUANIA

4

BATE BORISOV
- LATVIA
- SLOVAKIA
- BELARUS

5

WOLFSBERGER
- GERMANY
- AUSTRIA
- LUXEMBOURG

6
MARIBOR
- SWITZERLAND
- PORTUGAL
- SLOVENIA

7

FERENCVAROS
- HUNGARY
- GREECE
- CROATIA

8

NORRKOPING
- DENMARK
- FINLAND
- SWEDEN

9

RED STAR BELGRADE
- BOSNIA
- CROATIA
- SERBIA

MLS CROSSWORD!

Q Use the clues to fill the crossword – it's all about the USA's Major League Soccer!

ANSWERS ON P153 **MY SCORE** ☐ /10

MLS CROSSWORD!

Q Use the clues to fill the crossword – it's all about the USA's Major League Soccer!

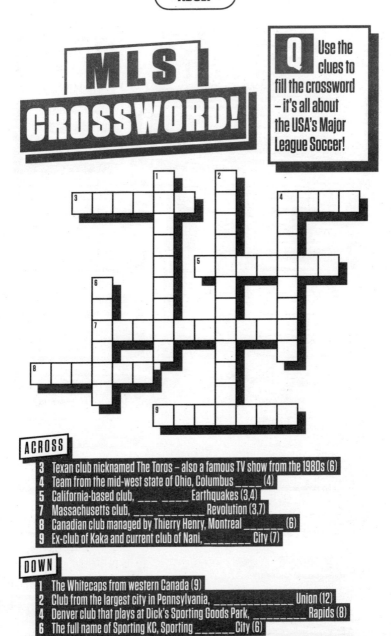

ACROSS

3 Texan club nicknamed The Toros – also a famous TV show from the 1980s (6)

4 Team from the mid-west state of Ohio, Columbus _____ (4)

5 California-based club, ____ ____ Earthquakes (3,4)

7 Massachusetts club, ____ _____ Revolution (3,7)

8 Canadian club managed by Thierry Henry, Montreal _____ (6)

9 Ex-club of Kaka and current club of Nani, _____ City (7)

DOWN

1 The Whitecaps from western Canada (9)

2 Club from the largest city in Pennsylvania, _____ Union (12)

4 Denver club that plays at Dick's Sporting Goods Park, _____ Rapids (8)

6 The full name of Sporting KC, Sporting _____ City (6)

CLUB & COUNTRY CONNECT!

1	ARGENTINA		A	CLUB AMERICA
2	AUSTRALIA		B	COLO-COLO
3	BRAZIL		C	SEONGNAM
4	CHILE		D	KASHIMA ANTLERS
5	CHINA		E	PALMEIRAS
6	COLOMBIA		F	SYDNEY
7	JAPAN		G	RIVER PLATE
8	MEXICO		H	GUANGZHOU EVERGRANDE
9	SOUTH KOREA		I	PENAROL
10	URUGUAY		J	ATLETICO NACIONAL

ANSWERS ON P153   **MY SCORE** ☐ **/10**

CLUB & COUNTRY CONNECT!

1	ARGENTINA	A	AL SADD
2	BRAZIL	B	BARCELONA SC
3	COLOMBIA	C	AL AHLY
4	ECUADOR	D	HEARTS OF OAK
5	EGYPT	E	FLAMENGO
6	GHANA	F	MAMELODI SUNDOWNS
7	QATAR	G	MILLONARIOS
8	SAUDI ARABIA	H	BURIRAM UNITED
9	SOUTH AFRICA	I	BOCA JUNIORS
10	THAILAND	J	AL HILAL

MESSI &
RONALDO

Congratulations – you've reached the final round. And, predictably, we've saved the best till last. Lionel Messi and Cristiano Ronaldo are undisputedly and undoubtedly the greatest players on planet earth – they've smashed record after record over the past decade. But how much do you know about these two footy icons? Showtime, quizzers!

BEAT THE CLOCK!

START•STOP
01:00
MIN   SEC

Q You've got 60 seconds to answer as many Messi and Ronaldo questions as you can!

1 Which ledge manager signed Cristiano Ronaldo for Man. United in 2003?

2 Which iconic megastar is older – Lionel Messi or Cristiano Ronaldo?

3 Which of the two players has won the Ballon d'Or award the most times?

4 One of them is the top Champions League scorer of all time – but which one?

5 Which of them scored in the 2009 and 2011 Champions League finals?

6 Which of the two superstars was born in a city called Rosario?

7 Which of the two has three children, called Thiago, Mateo and Ciro?

8 In which year did both players make their debut at a World Cup?

9 Who is the only player to win the Ballon d'Or ahead of Messi and Ronaldo since 2008?

10 Which PSG star shares a birthday – 5 February – with Cristiano Ronaldo?

ANSWERS ON P153   **MY SCORE** ⬜ /10

Q You've got 60 seconds to answer as many Messi and Ronaldo questions as you can!

1 Which manager handed Lionel Messi his La Liga debut for Barcelona?

....

2 How many times was Ronaldo PFA Player of the Year during his Man. United days?

....

3 Before the 2019-20 season, how many La Liga titles had Lionel Messi won in his career?

....

4 In which year did Lionel Messi make his debut for Argentina?

....

5 Which shirt number was Ronaldo given when he signed for Man. United?

....

6 Who was manager of Real Madrid when Ronaldo signed for the Spanish giants?

....

7 Which player was sent off on his international debut – Messi or Ronaldo?

....

8 How many times have they faced each other in a Champions League final?

....

9 Lionel Messi scored four goals against which English team back in 2010?

....

10 Who was youngest when they won their first Ballon d'Or – Messi or Ronaldo?

....

WHO'S YOUR TEAM-MATE?

Q Simple challenge – have these guys ever played in the same team as Messi or Ronaldo, or both?

1 GERARD PIQUE

MESSI
RONALDO
BOTH

2 ANGEL DI MARIA

MESSI
RONALDO
BOTH

3 GONZALO HIGUAIN

MESSI
RONALDO
BOTH

4 FABINHO

MESSI
RONALDO
BOTH

5 ADAMA TRAORE

MESSI
RONALDO
BOTH

6 ANDRE GOMES

MESSI
RONALDO
BOTH

7 KEYLOR NAVAS

MESSI
RONALDO
BOTH

8 PAULO DYBALA

MESSI
RONALDO
BOTH

9 THIAGO ALCANTARA

MESSI
RONALDO
BOTH

ANSWERS ON P153 **MY SCORE** /9

WHO'S YOUR TEAM-MATE?

Q Simple challenge – did these guys ever play in the same team as Messi or Ronaldo, or both?

1 HENRIK LARSSON

MESSI
RONALDO
BOTH

2 ZLATAN IBRAHIMOVIC

MESSI
RONALDO
BOTH

3 RONALDINHO

MESSI
RONALDO
BOTH

4 CARLOS TEVEZ

MESSI
RONALDO
BOTH

5 RICARDO QUARESMA

MESSI
RONALDO
BOTH

6 DIEGO FORLAN

MESSI
RONALDO
BOTH

7 EDWIN VAN DER SAR

MESSI
RONALDO
BOTH

8 DECO

MESSI
RONALDO
BOTH

9 DANI ALVES

MESSI
RONALDO
BOTH

ANSWERS ON P153 **MY SCORE** ☐ **/9**

THE ANSWERS

IT'S TIME TO CROWN THE MOTD MAG FAMILY FOOTY QUIZ BOOK CHAMPION!

THE FINAL SCORES

Add up all your scores from the 16 different rounds
to see who is OFFICIALLY your family's footy genius!

UNDER-16

[   ] /500

ADULT

[   ] /500

THE WINNER IS:

....

PREMIER LEAGUE

P10-11
LEAGUE OF NATIONS!

UNDER-16
1 Sadio Mane – Senegal
2 Richarlison – Brazil
3 Philip Billing – Denmark
4 Youri Tielemens – Belgium
5 Yerry Mina – Colombia
6 Fabian Schar – Switzerland
7 Josh King – Norway
8 Luka Milivojevic – Serbia
9 Jan Bednarek – Poland

ADULT
1 Juan Sebastian Veron – Argentina
2 Alexander Hleb – Belarus
3 Geremi – Cameroon
4 Juan Pablo Angel – Colombia
5 Davor Suker – Croatia
6 Sami Hyypia – Finland
7 Paulo Wanchope – Costa Rica
8 Lucas Radebe – South Africa
9 Marians Pahars – Latvia

P12-13
GOAL KINGS CROSSWORD!

UNDER-16
ACROSS
2 Watford 5 Chelsea
7 Sadio 9 Old Trafford
10 Gabon

DOWN
1 Harry Kane 3 Fleetwood
4 Mexico 6 Atletico
8 Abraham

ADULT
ACROSS
4 Monaco 5 Sutton
6 Real Madrid 7 Holland
9 Anelka
DOWN
1 Fowler 2 Southampton
3 Collymore 4 Marseille
8 Dion

P14-15
PFA TEAM OF THE YEAR TEASERS!

UNDER-16
2018-19
A L – Aymeric Laporte
B S – Bernardo Silva
P P – Paul Pogba
R S – Raheem Sterling
2017-18 K W – Kyle Walker
N O – Nicolas Otamendi
M A – Marcos Alonso
C E – Christian Eriksen
2016-17 K W – Kyle Walker
G C – Gary Cahill
E H – Eden Hazard
R L – Romelu Lukaku
2015-16 H B – Hector Bellerin
T A – Toby Alderweireld
R M – Riyad Mahrez
D P – Dimitri Payet

ADULT
1994-95 T F – Tim Flowers
R J – Rob Jones
G P – Gary Pallister
J K – Jurgen Klinsmann

1998-99 N M – Nigel Martyn
S C – Sol Campbell
E P – Emmanuel Petit
D G – David Ginola
2001-02
S G – Shay Given
S H – Sami Hyypia
W B – Wayne Bridge
R P – Robert Pires
2008-09
G J – Glen Johnson
N V – Nemanja Vidic
A Y – Ashley Young
N A – Nicolas Anelka

P16-17
BEAT THE CLOCK!

UNDER-16
1 Borussia Dortmund
2 Alan Shearer 3 Brazil
4 Oliver McBurnie
5 Southampton 6 Chelsea
7 Crystal Palace v Brighton
8 Man. United 9 Arsenal
10 MK Dons

ADULT
1 Brian Deane
2 Middlesbrough 3 Arsenal
4 Kenny Dalglish
5 Real Madrid 6 Holland
7 Man. City 8 Leeds
9 Arsenal 10 Tottenham

P18-19
GOLDEN BOYS!

UNDER-16
2009-10 Chelsea
2010-11 Man. United
2011-12 Arsenal
2012-13 Robin van Persie
2013-14 Luis Suarez

2014-15 Sergio Aguero
2015-16 Harry Kane
2016-17 Harry Kane
2017-18 Mohamed Salah
2018-19 Sadio Mane

ADULT
1992-93 Tottenham
1993-94 Newcastle
1994-95 Alan Shearer
1995-96 Blackburn
1996-97 Alan Shearer
1997-98 Michael Owen
1998-99 Leeds
1999-2000 Sunderland
2000-01 Jimmy Floyd Hasselbaink
2001-02 Thierry Henry

P20-21
PREMIER LEAGUE PERFORMERS!
UNDER-16
Bristol City – no
Oldham – yes
Bradford - yes
Brentford - no
Charlton – yes
Cardiff – yes
Coventry – yes
Derby – yes
Luton - no
QPR – yes
Notts County - no
Millwall – no
Swindon – yes
Sunderland – yes
Stoke – yes
Wigan – yes
Bolton – yes
Hull – yes
Reading – yes

Blackpool - yes

ADULT
Middlesbrough – yes
Blackburn – yes
Nottingham Forest – yes
Crystal Palace – yes
Watford - no
Leicester - no
Leeds – yes
Sheffield United – yes
West Brom – no
Newcastle – no
Southampton - yes
Man. City - yes
Ipswich - yes
Coventry - yes
Oldham - yes
Aston Villa - yes
Sheffield Wednesday - yes
QPR - yes
Norwich – yes
West Ham – no

WORLD CUP
P24-25
RUSSIA PUZZLER!
UNDER-16
1 Russia **2** Uruguay
3 Portugal **4** Denmark
5 Colombia **6** France
7 Mexico **8** Switzerland
9 Belgium

USA '94 FLASHBACK!
ADULT
1 Bulgaria **2** Austria
3 Colombia **4** Romania
5 Russia **6** Nigeria
7 Argentina **8** Switzerland
9 Sweden

P26-27
WORLD CUP WINNERS!
UNDER-16
WINNERS
2018 France **2014** Brazil
2010 Spain **2006** Germany
2002 Japan
GOLDEN BOOT WINNER
2018 Harry Kane
2014 Colombia
2010 Germany
2006 Germany
2002 Brazil

ADULT
WINNERS
1998 France
1994 USA
1990 Italy
1986 Argentina
1982 Italy
GOLDEN BOOT WINNER
1998 Davor Suker
1994 Bulgaria
1990 Toto Schillachi
1986 Gary Lineker
1982 Paolo Rossi

P28-29
WORLD CUP FINAL LOSERS!
UNDER-16
1 Argentina **2** Holland
3 France **4** Germany

ADULT
1 Brazil **2** Italy **3** Holland
4 Czechoslovakia

P30-31
BEAT THE CLOCK!
UNDER-16 1 Brazil **2** Croatia **3** German **4** 1966 **5** Mario Gotze **6** Pele **7** Gary Lineker **8** Marco Materazzi **9** 2006 **10** Luka Modric

ADULT 1 Uruguay **2** Brazil 2002 **3** Martin Peters **4** Andreas Brehme **5** Just Fontaine **6** Mario Kempes **7** Germany & Italy **8** Diana Ross **9** Jack Charlton **10** Andres Iniesta

P32 WORLD CUP KEEPERS!
UNDER-16 1 Russia **2** Chile **3** Croatia **4** Switzerland **5** Scotland **6** Germany **7** Brazil **8** Sweden **9** Uruguay

P33 HAT-TRICK HEROES!
ADULT 1 Argentina **2** Portugal **3** Russia **4** Czechoslovakia **5** Denmark **6** France **7** Hungary **8** Poland **9** Peru

CHAMPIONS LEAGUE

P36-37 CHAMPIONS MAP!
UNDER-16
1 F **2** K **3** L **4** H **5** J **6** A **7** I **8** G **9** E **10** B **11** D **12** C

ADULT
1 I **2** K **3** E **4** C **5** G **6** L **7** A **8** H **9** J **10** D **11** B **12** F

P38-39 LEGENDARY LINE-UPS!
UNDER-16
1 AC Milan **2** Barcelona **3** Inter Milan **4** Chelsea

ADULT 1 Ajax **2** Real Madrid **3** Porto **4** Marseille

P40-41 CAREER PATH!
UNDER-16
1 Robert Lewandowski **2** Luis Suarez **3** Gianlugi Buffon **4** Angel Di Maria

ADULT 1 Andriy Shevchenko **2** Pavel Nedved **3** Luis Figo **4** Marcel Desailly

P42-43 FINAL FANTASY!
UNDER-16
1 Barcelona **2** Juventus **3** Barcelona **4** Bayern Munich **5** Inter Milan

6 Chelsea **7** Atletico Madrid **8** Juventus **9** B. Dortmund
ADULT
1 Marseille **2** AC Milan **3** Ajax **4** Borussia Dortmund **5** Real Madrid **6** Real Madrid **7** Real Madrid **8** Liverpool **9** Porto

P44-45 BEAT THE CLOCK!
UNDER-16
1 Real Madrid **2** Cristiano Ronaldo **3** Germany **4** Sir Alex Ferguson **5** Wembley **6** Divock Origi **7** Inter Milan **8** Liverpool **9** Gareth Bale **10** Monaco

ADULT
1 Marseille **2** Nou Camp **3** Paul Lambert **4** David O'Leary **5** Mark Clattenburg **6** Roberto Di Matteo **7** Inter Milan **8** Ajax **9** Jens Lehmann **10** Wayne Rooney

P46 2019-20 LINE-UPS!
UNDER-16
1 Lyon **2** Ajax **3** Atletico Madrid **4** Napoli

P47 LEGENDARY LINE-UPS!

ADULT
1 Bayern Munich 2 Juventus
3 Monaco 4 Lazio

TRANSFERS
P50-51
TRANSFER RECORD PUZZLER!
UNDER-16
1 Neymar
2 Kylian Mbappe
3 Eden Hazard
4 Philippe Coutinho
5 Ousmane Dembele
6 Joao Felix
7 Antoine Griezmann
8 Paul Pogba
9 Cristiano Ronaldo
10 Gareth Bale

ADULT
1 Cristiano Ronaldo
2 Zlatan Ibrahimovic
3 Kaka
4 Zinedine Zidane
5 Luis Figo
6 Hernan Crespo
7 Gianluigi Buffon
8 Gaizka Mendieta
9 Juan Sebastian Veron
10 Christian Vieri

P52-53
CAREER PATH!
UNDER-16
1 Kevin De Bruyne – Chelsea
2 Sadio Mane
– Southampton
3 Mateo Kovacic

– Inter Milan
4 Toby Alderweireld
– Atletico Madrid

ADULT
1 Emmanuel Petit
– Barcelona
2 Nicky Butt – Newcastle
3 Jamie Redknapp
– Tottenham
4 Wim Jonk –
Sheffield Wednesday

FOOTBALL LEAGUE
P56-57
BADGE BAMBOOZLER!
UNDER-16
1 Wigan 2 Stoke
3 Derby 4 Charlton
5 Sunderland
6 Sheffield Wednesday
7 Middlesbrough
8 Plymouth 9 Coventry

ADULT
1 Salford 2 Oxford 3 Luton
4 Tranmere 5 Leyton Orient
6 Shrewsbury 7 Morecambe
8 Oldham 9 AFC Wimbledon

P58-59
LOCATION LOCATION LOCATION!
UNDER-16
1 Swansea – C

2 Middlesbrough – **A**
3 Birmingham – **E**
4 Charlton – **D**
5 Nottingham Forest – **F**
6 Luton – **B**

ADULT
1 Mansfield – **D**
2 MK Dons – **C**
3 Peterborough – **E**
4 Morecambe – **F**
5 Blackpool – **B**
6 Grimsby – **A**

P60-61
THE NICKMAME GAME!
UNDER-16
1 G 2 E 3 B 4 A 5 I
6 J 7 D 8 H 9 F 10 C
ADULT
1 F 2 J 3 H 4 G 5 E
6 D 7 A 8 I 9 C 10 B

P62-63
FOOTBALL LEAGUE SUPERSTARS!
UNDER-16
1 Aston Villa 2 Norwich
3 Leeds 4 Fulham
5 Shrewsbury
6 Sheffield United
7 MK Dons 8 Burnley
9 Coventry

ADULT
1 Oldham 2 Leeds
3 Wolves 4 Crewe
5 Bolton 6 Portsmouth

7 Preston **8** Gillingham
9 Watford

P64-65
STADIUM NAME GAME!
UNDER-16
1 Oakwell **2** St Andrew's
3 Ashton Gate **4** Deepdale
5 KCOM Stadium
6 Sixfields Stadium
7 Ewood Park
8 Portman Road
9 Fratton Park

ADULT
1 Highbury Stadium
2 Glanford Park
3 Priestfield Stadium
4 Keepmoat Stadium
5 Roots Hall
6 Sincil Bank
7 Valley Parade
8 Brunton Park
9 Spotland

WOMEN'S FOOTBALL
P68-69
GUESS WHO!
UNDER-16
1 Chloe Kelly
2 Lauren James
3 Steph Houghton
4 Beth England
5 Vivianne Miedema
6 Fara Williams
7 Ellie Roebuck
8 Gilly Flaherty

9 Leah Williamson

ADULT
1 Crystal Dunn **2** Sam Kerr
3 Marta **4** Christine Sinclair
5 Carly Telford
6 Eugenie Le Sommer
7 Sara Dabritz
8 Stina Blackstenius
9 Sari van Veenendaal

P70-71
WOMEN'S BALLER LINE-UPS!
UNDER-16
1 Man. City **2** Chelsea
3 Arsenal **4** Man. United

ADULT
1 USA **2** Spain
3 Japan **4** England

PREMIER LEAGUE 2
P74-75
PLAYER OF THE YEAR PUZZLER!
UNDER-16
2009-10 Wayne Rooney
2010-11 Gareth Bale
2011-12 Arsenal
2012-13 Tottenham
2013-14 Luis Suarez
2014-15 Eden Hazard
2015-16 Leicester
2016-17 N'Golo Kante
2017-18 Mohamed Salah
2018-19 Virgil van Dijk

ADULT
1992-93 Aston Villa
1993-94 Eric Cantona
1994-95 Blackburn
1995-96 Newcastle
1996-97 Newcastle
1997-98 Dennis Bergkamp
1998-99 David Ginola
1999-2000 Roy Keane
2000-01 Teddy Sheringham
2001-02 Ruud van Nistelrooy

P76-77
BEAT THE CLOCK!
UNDER-16
1 Roma **2** Selhurst Park
3 Portugal **4** Daniel Farke
5 Old Trafford
6 Sheffield United
7 Borussia Dortmund
8 Sir Alex Ferguson
9 Wayne Rooney
10 Man. City
ADULT
1 Middlesbrough **2** Man. City
3 Aston Villa **4** Everton
5 Coventry **6** Sunderland
7 West Ham **8** Birmingham
9 QPR **10** Glenn Hoddle

P78-79
GENERAL KNOWLEDGE CROSSWORD!
UNDER-16
ACROSS 2 Everton **4** Jota
7 Martial **8** Chris Wilder
9 Aymeric **10** Burnley
DOWN 1 Nigeria

3 Bournemouth 5 Highbury
6 David Moyes

ADULT
ACROSS 3 Ruel Fox
7 Emile Heskey **8** Coventry
9 Sherwood **10** Roy
DOWN 1 Warhurst
2 Southampton **4** Uwe
Rosler **5** Francis **6** Sharp

P80
2019-20
LINE-UPS!
UNDER-16
1 Brighton **2** Aston Villa
3 Sheffield United
4 Newcastle

P81
LEGENDARY
LINE-UPS!
ADULT 1 Middlesbrough
2 Bolton **3** Everton **4** Derby

P82-83
IT'S A TEAM
GAME!
UNDER-16 1 Burnley
2 Arsenal **3** Liverpool
4 Newcastle **5** Southampton
6 Tottenham **7** Man. City
8 Man. United **9** Chelsea
ADULT
1 Coventry **2** Chelsea
3 Tottenham **4** West Ham
5 Sheffield Wednesday
6 Derby **7** Newcastle
8 Coventry **9** Everton

P84-85
TITLE WINNERS WORDSEARCH!
SEVEN ANSWERS FOR EACH GRID

UNDER-16

ADULT

INTERNATIONAL
P88-89
BADGE

BAMBOOZLER!
UNDER-16
1 Spain **2** Brazil **3** Holland
4 Wales **5** Portugal
6 Argentina **7** Germany
8 Uruguay **9** Serbia

ADULT
1 Denmark 2 South Africa
3 Finland 4 Peru 5 Algeria
6 Turkey 7 Russia 8 Austria
9 Cameroon

P90-91
NATIONAL HEROES!

UNDER-16
1 Brazil 2 Sweden 3 Spain
4 Bosnia & Herzegovina
5 Colombia 6 Venezuela
7 Slovakia 8 Ukraine
9 Cameroon

ADULT
1 Iran 2 Czech Republic
3 Bermuda 4 Liberia
5 Benin 6 Nigeria
7 Trinidad & Tobago
8 Hungary 9 Ghana

P92-93
ENGLAND MISSING STARS!

UNDER-16
1 A Jordan Pickford
B Kyle Walker
C John Stones
D Harry Maguire
E Kieran Trippier
F Jordan Henderson
G Ashley Young
H Dele Alli
I Jesse Lingard
J Raheem Sterling
K Harry Kane

2 A Joe Hart B Kyle Walker
C Gary Cahill
D Chris Smalling
E Danny Rose F Dele Alli
G Eric Dier H Wayne Rooney
I Adam Lallana J Harry Kane
K Raheem Sterling

ADULT
1 A David Seaman
B Gareth Southgate
C Tony Adams
D Stuart Pearce
E Darren Anderton
F Paul Ince
G Steve McManaman
H David Platt
I Paul Gascoigne
J Teddy Sheringham
K Alan Shearer

2 A Peter Shilton
B Mark Wright C Paul Parker
D Des Walker E Terry Butcher
F Stuart Pearce G David Platt
H Paul Gascoigne
I Chris Waddle J Gary Lineker
K Peter Beardsley

P94-95
GENERAL KNOWLEDGE CROSSWORD!

UNDER-16
ACROSS
6 Copa 7 Windsor
8 Riyad Mahrez 9 Ryan Giggs
10 Griezmann

DOWN
1 Tartan 2 Portugal
3 Colombia 4 Norway

5 Roy Hodgson
ADULT
ACROSS
5 Poborsky 6 Enzo Scifo
7 Wales 8 Alan Shearer
9 Denmark 10 Scotland
DOWN
1 Bobby Robson 2 Armando
3 Pele 4 Jorge Campos

FA CUP
P98-99
FA CUP FINAL FLASHBACK!

UNDER-16
1 2018 2 2016 3 2015
4 2011 5 2013 6 2019

ADULT
1 1996 2 1990 3 2006
4 2001 5 2005 6 1987

P100-101
CUP FINAL GAFFERS!

UNDER-16
1 Pep Guardiola G Man. City
2 Antonio Conte C Chelsea
3 Arsene Wenger
D Arsenal
4 Louis van Gaal
J Man. United
5 Kenny Dalglish H Liverpool
6 Steve Bruce A Hull
7 Tim Sherwood B Aston Villa
8 Alan Pardew I C. Palace
9 Roberto Martinez E Wigan
10 Javi Gracia F Watford

ADULT
1 Joe Royle **E** Everton
2 Ruud Gullit **D** Chelsea
3 Rafael Benitez **G** Liverpool
4 Bobby Gould **A** Wimbledon
5 John Sillett **B** Coventry
6 Terry Venables
C Tottenham
7 Ron Atkinson
H Man. United
8 Bobby Robson **F** Ipswich
9 John Lyall **J** West Ham
10 Lawrie McMenemy
I Southampton

P102-103
CUP FINAL
MISSING MEN!
UNDER-16
2018-19
A Vincent Kompany
B Ilkay Gundogan
C Riyad Mahrez
2017-18
A Thibaut Courtois
B Cesc Fabregas
C Victor Moses
2016-17
A David Ospina
B Per Mertesacker
C Danny Welbeck
2016-17
A Daley Blind
B Michael Carrick
C Wayne Rooney

ADULT
1993-94
A Paul Parker
B Andrei Kanchelskis
C Mark Hughes
1987-88

A Lawrie Sanchez
B Vinnie Jones
C John Fashanu
1990-91
A Paul Stewart
B Paul Gascoigne
C Gary Lineker
1992-93
A Nigel Winterburn
B John Jensen
C Kevin Campbell

SCOTTISH
FOOTBALL
P106
BADGE
BAMBOOZLER!
UNDER-16
1 Rangers 2 Celtic
3 Hibernian 4 Aberdeen
5 Motherwell 6 Hearts
7 Kilmarnock 8 St Mirren
9 Dundee United

P107
OLD FIRM
TEASER!
ADULT
1 Rangers 2 Celtic
3 Rangers 4 Celtic
5 Rangers 6 Celtic
7 Celtic 8 Rangers
9 Rangers

P108-109
BEAT THE CLOCK!
UNDER-16
1 Celtic 2 Aberdeen

3 Hearts 4 Steven Gerrard
5 Celtic Park 6 Glasgow
7 Motherwell 8 Kilmarnock
9 Celtic 10 Aberdeen

ADULT
1 Aberdeen 2 Rangers
3 Finland 4 Brian Laudrup
5 Dundee United
6 Mark Viduka 7 Marco Negri
8 St Johnstone
9 Barcelona 10 Hibernian

LA LIGA/
SPAIN
P112-113
BARCA OR REAL?
UNDER-16
1 Both 2 Real 3 Barca
4 Barca 5 Real 6 Barca
7 Barca 8 Real 9 Real

ADULT
1 Both 2 Real 3 Barca
4 Both 5 Real 6 Barca
7 Barca 8 Both 9 Both

P114-115
BEAT THE CLOCK!
UNDER-16
1 Uruguay 2 Zinedine Zidane
3 Benfica 4 Barcelona
5 Lionel Messi 6 Espanyol
7 Japan 8 Mestalla
9 550 10 Villarreal

ADULT
1 Liverpool 2 Barcelona
3 Golden Ball 4 Qatar
5 Iker Casillas 6 Portugal

7 Deportivo La Coruna
8 Atletico Madrid
9 Espanyol **10** Juventus

P116-117
LEAGUE OF
NATIONS!
UNDER-16
1 Croatia **2** Wales
3 Slovenia **4** Argentina
5 Sweden **6** Cameroon
7 Denmark **8** Nigeria
9 France

ADULT
1 Uruguay **2** Italy
3 Finland **4** Nigeria
5 Mali **6** Holland
7 Argentina **8** South Africa
9 Mexico

P118-119
LA LIGA
CROSSWORD!
UNDER-16
ACROSS
5 Croatian **7** Liverpool
9 Real Sociedad
10 World Cup
DOWN
1 Kieran **2** Brazil **3** Espanyol
4 Sergio Ramos **6** Albiol
8 Man. City

ADULT
ACROSS
1 Serbia **4** Portuguese
5 Ferrer **8** Argentina
9 Uruguay **10** Puyol

DOWN
2 Alvaro Arbeloa **3** Koeman
6 Espanyol **7** Inter Milan

LIGUE 1/
FRANCE
P122-123
PLAYER OF THE
YEAR PUZZLER!
UNDER-16
2009-10 Argentina
2010-11 Eden Hazard
2014-15 Alexandre Lacazette
2016-17 Uruguay
2017-18 Neymar
2018-19 Kylian Mbappe

ADULT
1993-94 PSG
1995-96 Bordeaux
1996-97 Sonny Anderson
1997-98 Italy
1998-99 Ali Benarbia
1999-2000 Argentina

P124-125
PSG PUZZLER
CROSSWORD!
UNDER-16 – ACROSS
1 Beckham **4** Princes
5 Qatar **7** Cavani **8** Thiago
Silva **9** Verratti
DOWN
2 Costa Rica **3** Barcelona
6 Marseille **8** Tuchel

ADULT
ACROSS
1 Metz **4** Bordeaux **5** Papin

6 Waddle **7** Frank Leboeuf
9 Wiltord
DOWN
1 Monaco **2** Trezeguet
3 Juninho **8** Rai

BUNDESLIGA/
GERMANY
P128
GOLDEN BOYS!
UNDER-16
2009-10 Edin Dzeko
2011-12 Klaas-Jan Huntelaar
2012-13 Bayer Leverkusen
2013-14 Borussia Dortmund

P129
WHO AM I?
ADULT
1 Matthias Sammer **2** Lothar
Matthaus **3** Giovane Elber
4 Lucio

P130-131
LEAGUE OF
NATIONS!
UNDER-16
1 Canada **2** Switzerland
3 Austria **4** Norway
5 Jamaica **6** Italy **7** Belgium
8 Togo **9** Holland

ADULT
1 Ivory Coast **2** Belgium
3 Bulgaria **4** Venezuela
5 Nigeria **6** Croatia **7** USA
8 Czech Republic
9 Australia

SERIE A/ITALY
P134
BADGE BAMBOOZLER!
UNDER-16
1 Atalanta 2 Juventus
3 Lazio 4 Inter Milan
5 AC Milan 6 Roma
7 Sampdoria 8 Fiorentina
9 Bologna

P135
SERIE A RETRO STARS!
ADULT 1 Luis Oliveira
2 Angelo Di Livio
3 Lilian Thuram
4 Sinisa Mihajlovic
5 Nestor Sensini
6 Marcelo Salas
7 Pavel Nedved 8 Rui Costa
9 Giuseppe Signori

P136-137
CAREER PATH!
UNDER-16 1 Giorgio Chiellini
2 Aaron Ramsey
3 Cristiano Ronaldo
4 Gonzalo Higuain

ADULT
1 Paul Elliott 2 Des Walker
3 Ashley Cole 4 David Platt

THE GLOBAL GAME

P140-141
COUNTRY CHALLENGE!
UNDER-16
1 Croatia 2 Switzerland
3 Holland 4 Russia 5 Turkey
6 Greece 7 Ukraine 8 Spain
9 Republic Of Ireland

ADULT
1 Denmark 2 Romania
3 Bulgaria 4 Belarus
5 Austria 6 Slovenia
7 Hungary 8 Sweden
9 Serbia

P142-143
MLS CROSSWORD!
UNDER-16
ACROSS
1 United 3 Inter 6 New York
8 Chicago 9 Real
10 Sounders
DOWN 2 Toronto 4 Houston
5 Timbers 7 Galaxy

ADULT
3 Dallas 4 Crew 5 San Jose
7 New England 8 Impact
9 Orlando
DOWN
1 Vancouver 2 Philadelphia
4 Colorado 6 Kansas

P144-145
CLUB & COUNTRY CONNECT!
UNDER-16

1 G 2 F 3 E 4 B 5 H
6 J 7 D 8 A 9 C 10 I

ADULT
1 I 2 E 3 G 4 B 5 C
6 D 7 A 8 J 9 F 10 H

MESSI & RONALDO
P148-149
BEAT THE CLOCK!
UNDER-16
1 Sir Alex Ferguson
2 Ronaldo 3 Messi
4 Ronaldo 5 Messi 6 Messi
7 Messi 8 2006 9 Luka
Modric 10 Neymar

ADULT
1 Frank Rijkaard 2 Twice
3 Ten 4 2005
5 No.7 6 Manuel Pellegrini
7 Messi 8 Once – 2009 final
9 Arsenal 10 Messi

P150-151
WHO'S YOUR TEAM-MATE?
UNDER-16
1 Both 2 Both 3 Both
4 Ronaldo 5 Messi 6 Both
7 Ronaldo 8 Both 9 Messi

ADULT
1 Both 2 Messi
3 Messi 4 Both
5 Ronaldo 6 Ronaldo
7 Ronaldo 8 Both 9 Messi